T0255100

SpringerBriefs in Cybersecurity

Cybersecurity is a difficult and complex field. The technical, political and legal questions surrounding it are complicated, often stretching a spectrum of diverse technologies, varying legal bodies, different political ideas and responsibilities. Cybersecurity is intrinsically interdisciplinary, and most activities in one field immediately affect the others. Technologies and techniques, strategies and tactics, motives and ideologies, rules and laws, institutions and industries, power and money—all of these topics have a role to play in cybersecurity, and all of these are tightly interwoven.

The SpringerBriefs in Cybersecurity series is comprised of two types of briefs: topic- and country-specific briefs. Topic-specific briefs strive to provide a comprehensive coverage of the whole range of topics surrounding cybersecurity, combining whenever possible legal, ethical, social, political and technical issues. Authors with diverse backgrounds explain their motivation, their mindset, and their approach to the topic, to illuminate its theoretical foundations, the practical nuts and bolts and its past, present and future. Country-specific briefs cover national perceptions and strategies, with officials and national authorities explaining the background, the leading thoughts and interests behind the official statements, to foster a more informed international dialogue.

More information about this series at http://www.springer.com/series/10634

Martin Schallbruch · Isabel Skierka

Cybersecurity in Germany

Springer

Martin Schallbruch
Digital Society Institute
European School of Management
  and Technology
Berlin, Germany

Isabel Skierka
Digital Society Institute
European School of Management
  and Technology
Berlin, Germany

ISSN 2193-973X   ISSN 2193-9748   (electronic)
SpringerBriefs in Cybersecurity
ISBN 978-3-319-90013-1   ISBN 978-3-319-90014-8   (eBook)
https://doi.org/10.1007/978-3-319-90014-8

Library of Congress Control Number: 2018946668

Printed on acid-free paper

This Springer imprint is published by the registered company Springer International Publishing AG
part of Springer Nature
The registered company address is: Gewerbestrasse 11, 6330 Cham, Switzerland

Foreword

Germany is certainly one of the more interesting countries when it comes to national cyberpolicies. It has been engaged in data privacy and information security since the very early days of commercial computing. Its federal institutions, crafting and implementing computer security technologies, laws, standards, and rules, are more than twenty years old, and the country's public discourse about privacy and security started in the 1980s and is still very much alive and emotional. And yet while Germany did not really come up with good answers on how to actually solve the cybersecurity problem at large either, it is an interesting place to look at— especially for lessons learned.

But to actually assess lessons learned in Germany, those lessons would have to be marked as such. This is difficult. Germany has a very bad culture regarding errors, especially in the government. There is a saying among German ministries: The ministry never makes a mistake. In other words, if you make a mistake anyhow —which is absolutely inevitable in an area as complex as cybersecurity and rather the rule than the exception—it should still look like a success. That renders learning a tedious and difficult enterprise for those who have not actually been a part of the learning curve.

Lucky for this SpringerBrief, both authors were and are part of the German learning curve and can provide the readers with "inside" insights. Martin Schallbruch and Isabel Skierka are both close participants and watchers of cyber-security policies in Germany. As former and longtime Ministerial Director of the Federal Ministry of the Interior, Martin Schallbruch has effectively been in charge as both strategist and implementer of most of Germany's previous governmental efforts in cybersecurity. He has overseen the Federal Office for Information Security (Bundesamt für Sicherheit in der Informationstechnik) and was instrumental in the design of a variety of laws governing cybersecurity in Germany. Now being a scientist, his many firsthand experiences provide a wealth of empirical material on many of the otherwise hidden nuts and bolts of the creation of governance in this area, of wins and losses, imperceptible difficulties, and unearthed options. Isabel Skierka complements this experience with a brilliant and inquisitive scientific mind and her own set of many years of close encounters with cybersecurity policy-making as a governmental advisor and researcher, providing an external perspective. In addition, Isabel Skierka has always been very active in the two other policy fields apart from interior security which were of high relevance in Germany's path in cyberpolicy: defense and foreign policy.

Accordingly, both authors together form a perfect team to describe, analyze, and assess cybersecurity policy-making in Germany, and this is very much reflected in the SpringerBrief.

And they span the entire spectrum of relevant events, structures, perspectives, and actors. They start out by explaining the peculiarities of the German mindset around anything informational and security-based, and the impact these public perspectives had and still have on policy-making. From there, they brilliantly explore the entire history and evolution of Germany's cybersecurity strategy, providing and explaining the main documents, how they came into existence, and how (or in some cases: why not) they have been implemented. These excellent explanations are most valuable as they critically explore the many mundane, yet highly relevant problems stemming from government rivalries, industry influence, and political agendas—elements, which seem negligible to many outsiders, but which actually form the very heart of the lack of progress in many cases of particular policies, initiatives, or technologies. Following these historical explanations, they deepen their systematic analysis of persistent gaps and problems and project their insights on current and evolving policy fields for cybersecurity, some of them again very typically German, predicting (no doubt with high certainty) upcoming problems in the creation of policies for these new areas.

As editor, I am highly pleased and in fact proud of this particular volume, as it does a perfect job at, first, providing an in-depth and otherwise imperceptible look into the hidden secret dynamics of cybersecurity in Germany, and, second, such a brilliant systematic analysis of this particular history, which provides a ton of highly valuable insights for any researcher or practitioner in cybersecurity strategy.

Berlin, Germany   Dr. Sandro Gaycken
May 2018

Contents

Chapter 1
Introduction

Abstract This Springer Brief provides an analysis of the evolution of cybersecurity policy in Germany over the past two an a half decades. The introduction explains the terminological and methodological principles of the work and outlines the structure of the Brief.

Keyword Cybersecurity · Germany

With the digitisation of nearly all aspects of life, our societies increasingly depend on the resilience and security of computing and communication technologies. Hence, the protection of information technology (IT) against unauthorised access, attack, and accidental failure, has become a priority for nation-states around the world.

Throughout the past one or two decades, most countries have adopted strategies, policies and practical steps to protect the security of IT and critical infrastructures within their territory, and, by extension, their citizens. These practices are generally subsumed under the umbrella of cybersecurity.

The resulting development of various national cybersecurity perspectives and policies is covered by this dedicated Springer series. This Springer Brief provides an analysis of the evolution of cybersecurity policy in Germany over the past two and a half decades.

1.1 On Terminology

As a policy field, cybersecurity is still comparatively young, with most nations having started to adopt national cybersecurity policy documents and strategies only a decade ago. In fact, the very definition of the term "cybersecurity" remains unclear and the concept itself remains contested (Wagner and Vieth 2016). Each national context will define the specific definitions and approaches to the challenges and opportunities related to it (Hathaway and Klimburg 2012; Global Cyber Definitions Database 2018).

© The Author(s) 2018
M. Schallbruch and I. Skierka, *Cybersecurity in Germany*, SpringerBriefs
in Cybersecurity, https://doi.org/10.1007/978-3-319-90014-8_1

Cybersecurity is closely related to concepts such as IT security, which refers to the confidentiality, integrity, and availability of information, and information assurance, computer security, and network security. However, IT security is only one technical aspect of cybersecurity.

Cybersecurity encompasses technologies, processes, and policies that help to prevent or reduce the negative impact of events in cyberspace that can happen as the result of deliberate actions against IT by a malevolent actor (Computer Science and Telecommunications Board 2014; Tabansky and Ben Israel 2015). These processes and associated practices differ across organizations and geographic regions.

The term "cybersecurity" was not used in official German government documents until the first cybersecurity strategy in 2011. Earlier documents mostly refer to "IT security" or "critical information infrastructure security", which are more technical in scope than cybersecurity. This Brief will consistently use the term "cybersecurity policy" in order to refer to the overall development of this policy area. Whenever it refers to particular documents and developments, it will use the terminology employed by policy-makers.

1.2 Approach

The description and analysis of German cybersecurity policy is based on the evaluation of a variety of official documents released by German government agencies, as well as news articles and international policy documents. In addition, it draws on academic literature and policy analyses in the field of cybersecurity, data protection, and national security more generally. The Brief further focuses on institutional arrangements and corresponding federal and state laws. It benefits from co-author's Martin Schallbruch's first-hand experience in cybersecurity policy-making in the federal government, as well as from both co-authors' experience with academic and policy research and consultancy activities in the field, most recently at the Digital Society Institute of the European School for Management and Technology Berlin.

1.3 Peculiarities of the German Political System

Every country's politics and political system are unique. In the post-World War II period, Germany was a divided country until 1990. Its historical past—the Nazi era and the Communist East German regime with its Stasi secret police—are ever present in politics and society. The Nazi regime systematically abused private data for the identification and persecution of Jews, homosexuals, political opponents, and other groups. East Germany functioned as a socialist dictatorship in which the Stasi ran a nationwide surveillance regime that relied on denunciation and electronic surveillance. Not least because of the lessons of this past, the German public and policy-makers attach so much importance to data protection and privacy (Freude and Freude 2016).

Readers should take into account two additional aspects of the German political system while reading this Brief: German federalism and coalition government.

Germany's political system is based on federalism, a system of government in which power is shared between the central state (at the federal level) and federal regional states. The German federal system comprises sixteen federal states, so-called "Länder". Each state has its own government, headed by a minister president. At the national federal level, the sixteen Länder are represented by the German Federal Council (Bundesrat), which has a vital legislative role in passing new legislative initiatives, even those proposed by the federal government.

Cybersecurity is mainly dealt with as a national policy issue in Germany, although most states have some form of administrative IT security structures in place. When it comes to cyber crime and counter espionage, law enforcement agencies at the state level play an essential role. Law enforcement in Germany is constitutionally vested at the federal level and with the states, which each have their own police agencies and offices for the protection of the constitution (domestic intelligence agencies).

Finally, governments in Germany are almost always formed by party alliances, so-called coalition governments. In following, this Brief repeatedly refers to national government coalition "agreements" or "treaties". These are the political agendas which coalition parties negotiate before taking office after federal elections. The coalition treaties constitute important official documents that indicate government priorities and against which a coalition government's achievements will be evaluated. The most recent coalition treaty dates from March 2018, when the CDU, its sister party CSU, and the SPD started governing.

1.4 Structure

In following, this Brief analyses public perspectives on cybersecurity, government strategies, national organizational aspects, as well as an outlook on gaps and priorities in Germany's cybersecurity policy. The remaining chapters are structured as follows:

- Chapter 2 provides an overview of the public perspective on the challenges, strategies, and instruments of cybersecurity in Germany. It illuminates the link between data protection and cybersecurity issues in the public debate, the emergence of particular political and regulatory concepts dealing with IT and cybersecurity, and the debate about "digital sovereignty" resulting from the revelations of former US National Security Agency contractor Edward Snowden.
- Chapter 3 traces the evolution of German cybersecurity strategy throughout the past two and a half decades in historically chronological order. It describes and analyses various cybersecurity strategy and policy documents. Thereby, the chapter illustrates the increasingly comprehensive scope of German cybersecurity policy, whose emphasis has broadened from a civilian defence perspective to include international diplomatic and strategic military aspects in recent years.

- Chapter 4 explains the national organization of cybersecurity responsibilities and corresponding institutions in Germany. It focuses on cooperation and conflict between government agencies, and on public-private cooperation in cybersecurity.
- Chapter 5 presents an evaluation of current gaps in German cybersecurity policy which the government will need to address in the upcoming years. It considers six fields of action: active cyber defence, the national cybersecurity architecture, the state's handling of IT security vulnerabilities, Germany's and Europe's industrial IT security policy, the legal framework for IT security liability, and Germany's cooperation with international partners.
- Chapter 6 provides concluding remarks to this Brief.

References

Computer Science and Telecommunications Board (2014) At the nexus of cybersecurity and public policy some basic concepts and issues. The National Academy of Sciences

Freude A, Freude T (2016) Echoes of history: understanding German data protection. Bertelsmann Foundation

Global Cyber Definitions Database (2018) New America. http://cyberdefinitions.newamerica.org/

Hathaway M, Klimburg A (2012) Preliminary considerations: on national cyber security. In: National cyber security framework manual. NATO Cooperative Cyber Defence Centre of Excellence, Tallinn, pp 1–43

Tabansky L, Ben Israel I (2015) Cybersecurity in Israel. Springer Nature, London

Wagner B, Vieth K (2016) Was macht cyber? Epistemologie und Funktionslogik von Cyber. Zeitschrift für Außen- und Sicherheitspolitik 9:213–222

Chapter 2
The German View on Cybersecurity

Abstract The German public perspective on the challenges, procedures, and instruments of cybersecurity follows three lines of development: First, the close link of cybersecurity with data protection and privacy issues; second, the distinct way of dealing with technical hazards by means of (regulatory and engineering) risk prevention mechanisms; and third, the debate on "digital sovereignty" that was triggered by the Snowden revelations.

Keywords Data protection · Privacy · Legal concepts · Risk prevention
Digital sovereignty · Snowden

2.1 The Public Perception of Cyber Issues

Public attention for cybersecurity in Germany first emerged in the context of successful hacking attacks. Since the 1980s, (western) Germany has been home to a very active hacking community around the Chaos Computer Club (CCC) in Hamburg, an association founded in 1981. The CCC succeeded at an early stage in reaching a broad public with successful hacking attacks. They conducted their first notable hack in 1984 by manipulating the so-called "Btx" system, a teletext system operated by the national postal service. The CCC demonstrated how it could hack the "Hamburger Sparkasse" bank's system and steal 135,000 Deutsche Mark [former German currency unit (Oppliger 1992, p. 18)]. The CCC returned the money but had successfully demonstrated the substantial risks of banks' insecure computer systems for customers. Another hacker group associated with the CCC offered their expertise and services to the Russian intelligence service KGB from 1985 onwards. In return for payment, the group penetrated militarily relevant computer systems, including those of the American military, and provided the information to the KGB (Ammann 1989, Stoll 1989).

© The Author(s) 2018
M. Schallbruch and I. Skierka, *Cybersecurity in Germany*, SpringerBriefs
in Cybersecurity, https://doi.org/10.1007/978-3-319-90014-8_2

From the very beginning, the German public perception of hacking has been ambivalent: On the one hand, successful hacks raised awareness for the risks of information technology (IT) for users, especially concerning data privacy. At the same time, hacking was considered a new form of crime and raised considerable concerns among the population. As a result, Germany was one of the first countries to make hacking a criminal offense in 1986. However, the then introduced § 202a of the penal code only criminalized the theft of data, but not the intrusion into a system under surpassing security precautions. The German parliament wanted to avoid "over-criminalization" of hacking (Winkelbauer 1986, p. 488). In line with the implementation of the 2001 Convention on Cybercrime of the Council of Europe into national law, Germany had to extend its criminal law. Since 2007, "mere hacking", i.e. intrusion into protected computer systems, has also been punishable by law (Schreibauer and Hessel 2007).

Before the turn of the millennium, however, successful hacking attacks were hardly seen as significant threats. The public perception changed with the year 2000 when users became widely concerned about the availability of the computer systems in the context of the "Year 2000" or "Y2K" problem. The Y2K problem refers to a class of computer bugs related to the formatting and storage of calendar data that was projected to create havoc in computers and computer networks around the world at the beginning of the year 2000 (Encyclopedia Britannica 2018).

In anticipation of the risk, the government assigned high priority to the preparation of computer systems for the turn of the millennium. It prepared citizens by distributing information mail to all households and set up a comprehensive crisis management plan to assure the government's ability to act in case the risk would materialize. Ultimately, few failures occurred in the transition from December 31, 1999, to January 1, 2000. What remained of the Y2K bug was an increased sensitivity for questions of computer security (Bundesministerium für Wirtschaft und Energie 1999).

As a result, the increasingly frequent occurrence of cyber attacks triggered growing public reactions—starting with the Loveletter virus, which spread explosively via E-mail attachments in May 2000. The incident led to a first intensive debate about cybersecurity in the German Bundestag. Since the Loveletter virus exclusively affected Microsoft products, the discussion focused strongly on the question of the security relevance of a "Microsoft monoculture" (Deutscher Bundestag 2000, p. 9541D ff.). In the wake of the incidents, the reduction of the government's, industry's, and society's dependency on Microsoft products and support for open source alternatives became a more or less vigorously pursued policy goal of the federal government.

Around the turn of the millennium, public attention concentrated on the reliability of IT. This focus shifted in the following years. The threat of cyber attacks for the confidentiality and integrity of data became more and more relevant. The traditionally high degree of attention of the German public for data protection and privacy aspects overshadowed cybersecurity issues. The media and public voices framed major hacks such as the theft of data of 17 million customers from Deutsche Telekom in 2006 foremost as data protection problems (Deutsche Welle 2008).

2.2 Political and Regulatory Concepts

The regulatory concepts for the protection of cybersecurity in Germany are closely linked to the protection of personal data. Even before the concept of "information security" emerged in the early 1980s, "data security" had been a legal obligation. Already the first Federal Data Protection Act of 1977, in Section 6, included mandatory legal responsibilities to take technical and organizational steps to protect data. Since then, this obligation has applied to all companies and authorities that process personal data on computer systems. A catalogue annexed to the act provides a rough description of the measures, from which the protection goals of confidentiality and integrity of the data can already be deduced (Gesetz zum Schutz vor Mißbrauch personenbezogener Daten bei der Datenverarbeitung as of January 27, 1977). Until today, there are no significant differences in the ways information security and data security are technically implemented. Although data protection and IT security have different legal bases in the EU, the EU General Data Protection Regulation (EU GDPR) (GDPR EU 2016) on the one hand and the EU Directive on Network and Information Security (NIS Directive) (NIS Directive EU 2016) on the other, their respective technical implementation is similar.

Data security and information security laws are rooted in the regulatory concept of German technology law, which in turn originates from the environmental law but has meanwhile dispersed to a wide range of other fields of law. Following German technology law, the handling of "dangerous" technologies, i.e. systems that have potentially harmful effects on humans (and the environment), requires governmental approval, which is given only under particular (technical) conditions. This idea was transferred to the electronic data processing: Just as the operation of power plants is prohibited, unless the law and directives stipulate requirements for smoke purification and/or related requirements, data protection law prohibits the processing of personal data via IT systems, unless the systems meet specific technical data security requirements. Risks arising from the use of technology are to be reduced to such an extent through technical and organizational measures that the remaining residual risk is acceptable for humans, the environment, and society as a whole.

The definition of IT systems requirements in data protection law supplements the additional legal question of whether the data may be processed at all for a respective purpose. The systems must comply with appropriate data security measures. In this context, German (and European) data protection law typically focuses on "state of the art" security. The idea behind this reference is to ensure that the implementation of security measures is not planned statically but is designed and updated dynamically on a long-term basis in a risk-adequate manner (Michaelis 2016).

Given the similarity of data protection and cybersecurity in the German political debate, it is not surprising that the concept of technology law, which the data protection law already reflects, has also been adopted in the area of IT security law. The first German cybersecurity-related strategy, the 2005 National Plan for the Protection of Information Infrastructures (Bundesministerium des Innern 2005), already focuses on the preventive protection of systems against cyber attacks. Two outstanding events were catalysts for the creation of the strategy. On the one hand, the 9/11 attacks in the United States (US) led the German government to subject Germany's security architecture under extensive scrutiny from 2002 onwards. The overhaul included—for the first time—the security of information infrastructures. In several studies, the government identified the level of protection of IT systems in Germany's most important infrastructures and recognized significant needs for improving preventive protection measures (Bundesministerium des Innern 2004, p. 246). The second motive for the government's action was a denial of service attack on the federal government's networks in 2004, which led to considerable disruptions of digital collaboration within the government. The government networks were flooded with irrelevant e-mails. This attack considerably restricted the usual e-mail communication of the authorities (Schulze 2006, p. 137).

Another aspect illustrating German cybersecurity policy's emphasis on technical requirements for IT systems and the technical handling of cyber attacks is the growing role of the Federal Office for Information Security (Bundesamt für Sicherheit in der Informationstechnik, BSI) throughout the past two decades. Founded as a licensing and certification authority for cryptographic systems and for eavesdropping defence purposes, the agency has meanwhile become a special police authority for all questions of IT security. Its competencies range from the investigation of IT products and the supervision of critical infrastructures to the investigation and defence of cyber attacks on governmental and critical infrastructures. With the federal cybersecurity strategy of 2011, the agency even became the lead body of the cyber defence centre, which connects all German cybersecurity authorities (Bundesministerium des Innern 2011).

The engineering approach of the BSI, the development and use of technically secured systems, became an essential constant of German cybersecurity policy. The Federal Constitutional Court also contributed to this development. Asked about the conditions under which state authorities can use trojan software to penetrate into the computer systems of terrorist suspects, the court created a new fundamental right derived from the German constitution to guarantee the integrity and confidentiality of information technology systems, which was then also referred to as the "fundamental right to IT security" (Bundesverfassungsgericht 2008; Hornung 2008). It juxtaposes the right of informational self-determination, the constitutional legal basis of German data protection, with a similarly constructed fundamental right to security of IT systems against state intervention. For each case in which governmental measures invade private ICT systems, referred to as "lawful hacking", a legal basis and appropriate technical and organizational security measures are required. Lawmakers have to change a national security law to define the circumstances, under which police forces and intelligence services are entitled to lawful hacking. The constitutional court also adopted the concept of primary technical protection of IT security: in cases of considerable risks to national or individual security, the state may hack IT systems. Yet, the risks to the security of the respective IT system must be reduced, by technological measures, to such an a tolerable level.

2.3   Snowden and the Emerging Discussion About Technological Sovereignty

The revelations of materials by Edward Snowden in 2013, which documented the US National Security Agency's (NSA) and other "Five Eye" alliance intelligence agency's surveillance activities in Europe, were particularly relevant to Germany. Virtually overnight, the revelations lifted cybersecurity from the realm of technocratic politics up onto the government's top political agenda. The German public had already historically been sensitive to data protection issues. Policymakers carefully followed the disclosures about the National Security Agency's (NSA) methods, which began with reports about the PRISM surveillance programme[1] (Gellman and Poitras 2013). Furthermore, it quickly became clear that German citizens, companies, and politicians were also directly affected by the NSA's surveillance. The debate reached its climax with the announcement in October 2013 that the NSA had surveilled the cell phone of German Chancellor Angela Merkel. Finally, the disclosures revealed another set of facts: the German intelligence services had cooperated with and supported the NSA's electronic surveillance activities. In particular, the Foreign Intelligence Service (Bundesnachrichtendienst, BND) had collaborated closely with the NSA in monitoring international telecommunications on German territory (Rosenbach and Stark 2014; Deutscher Bundestag 2017). According to German constitutional law experts, the BND practice of collecting foreign communication data infringed upon the right to private communication guaranteed by Article 10 of the German Basic Law. This right protects every person independent of her citizenship or country of residence (Bäcker 2014; Wetzling 2016).

Edward Snowden's publications put German political decision-makers under pressure to provide answers to crucial questions: Do US intelligence services access German domestic digital communications? To what extent are data of German citizens protected on the servers of American companies? How safe are German companies from US industrial espionage? Are the government's communication networks and communications resources adequately secured? Are IT products and digital services from US companies still trustworthy? And above all, what can future cooperation on cybersecurity issues with the US look like after this loss of confidence? The reports on NSA activities acted as an accelerator for German cyber politics. In the run-up to federal elections for a new German parliament (Bundestag) in the fall of 2013, data protection and cybersecurity became critical campaign issues. Chancellor Angela Merkel quickly presented an 8-point programme for enhanced privacy protection (Bundesministerium des Innern und Bundesministerium für Wirtschaft und Energie 2013; Funke 2013).

The adopted initiatives not only put intelligence cooperation with the US under scrutiny. The Federal Government also announced a speeding-up of European data protection legislation, including elevated standards for data transfer to the USA and

---

[1]PRISM is a code name for a programme under which the US NSA collected internet communications from various U.S. internet companies, including Microsoft, Yahoo, Google, Facebook, PalTalk, AOL, Skype, YouTube, and Apple.

other non-EU states. What was new in the government's official policy was the idea to strengthen the national (and European) IT industry to be able to use trustworthy products and services from Europe and to reduce their dependency on US providers (Bundesministerium des Innern und Bundesministerium für Wirtschaft und Energie 2013, pp. 6–7). A government-led roundtable on "Security Technology in the IT sector" with representatives from all levels of government, industry, and academia elaborated a wide range of measures to promote the development and use of trust-worthy IT systems (Bundesministerium des Innern et al. 2013).

The Snowden revelations also had an impact on the programme of the newly elected federal government in autumn 2013. Never before and never since has a coalition agreement to form a German government included such a comprehensive agenda on cybersecurity. The government coalition parties agreed on the adoption of an IT security law, as well as on the strengthening of the Federal Office for Information Security's (BSI) role in cybersecurity. For the first time, Germany's coalition agreement also calls for "regaining Germany's technological sovereignty". The idea behind this call for action was to introduce technical, legal, and political measures to better protect citizens, industry, and state authorities from surveillance by foreign intelligence agencies. The deployment of trustworthy national IT security technology should provide greater protection for citizens. The coalition treaty even brought up the idea of implementing national or 'Schengen' routing for discussion, i.e. redesigning the Internet infrastructures in such a way that data remains within Germany or Europe (CDU et al. 2013, p. 148ff.).

Political decision makers' call for regaining "technological sovereignty" in Germany and Europe subsequently developed into a broader political agenda. Apart from the 2013 coalition treaty, the German government's "Digital Agenda" of 2014 emphasised the government's plan to consider Germany's technological sovereignty in its external trade policy (Bundesregierung 2014).

Despite their extensive use in public discourse, to this date technological or digital sovereignty remain ill-defined concepts. Instead, they are political expressions being used to justify a range of measures under the umbrella of counter-surveillance and espionage. These include the overcoming of dependencies on foreign IT components (Eckert 2013, Bitkom 2015), the creation of independence of own telecommunications networks from foreign servers, so that internal data traffic would not leave German jurisdiction, as well as the equipment of national intelligence agencies with better capabilities to be at eye level with foreign intelligence agencies (Schaar 2015). As a result, the government has taken some actions to strengthen and facilitate the use of German technologies, such as research funding programmes or changes in procurement practices. In individual cases, the government terminated service contracts with US providers and replaced them with German providers, such as the US company Verizon's services for the German government network (Deutscher Bundestag 2017, p. 336ff.; Hathaway 2014, p. 302).

More recently, the term has mostly been used to refer to measures to enhance data protection and informational self-determination of individual citizens.

With the development of an IT security law, which was initiated directly at the start of the new government's work, Germany has become a European pioneer in the regulation of cybersecurity. The German law came into force in summer 2015 (Gesetz zur Erhöhung der Sicherheit informationstechnischer Systeme (IT-Sicherheitsgesetz) vom 17. Juli 2015), the corresponding EU Network Information Security directive followed only one year later. The boost to Germany's cybersecurity policy resulting from the Snowden revelations had a considerable impact on policy-making in the 18th parliamentary term from 2013 to 2017, even though it did not implement all agreed measures in the end (Schallbruch et al. 2018).

2.4 Combining a German Data Protection and Engineering Approach with Holistic Cyber Debates

For many years, the German discussion on cybersecurity has been limited to questions of data protection, technical and organizational security of IT systems and criminal prosecution in cyberspace. At the same time, the debate on internet policy had already been in full swing since 2005, which even led to the emergence of a new political party, the Pirate Party, which was very successful for some years (Lauer and Lobo 2015). However, this debate had little impact on cybersecurity policy. Issues of data protection, copyright law, the blocking of illegal content on the Internet, access to metadata by security agencies or the provision of open data were far more in the focus of internet policy (including the politics of the Pirate Party) than the discussion of how Germany should defend itself, its citizens, and critical infrastructures in cyberspace. Nor did Germany develop international political visibility in the field of cybersecurity.

Although IT and cybersecurity are focus areas of digital policy as outlined in the Federal Government's Digital Agenda for the years 2014–2017, the Agenda emphasises a technical approach of data and system protection, supplemented by the expansion of law enforcement capabilities in the digital realm. Technology policy approaches to strengthening national technological sovereignty remain unclear, and the Agenda lacks a more holistic view on cybersecurity with a regard to international security, global competitiveness, and human rights (Bundesregierung 2014).

The more extensive opening-up of cybersecurity policy did not occur until the military's late entry into the German cyber domain. For many years, the armed forces (Bundeswehr) had not developed its own cybersecurity policy. Instead, it was a contributing party within the civil cybersecurity strategies of the Interior Ministry. In 2014–2015, the Ministry of Defence started to develop its own cyber strategy. With the establishment of a Command for Cyber and Information Space (Kommando Cyber- und Informationsraum, CIR), the reorganization of the ministry and other supporting measures such as the establishment of Cybersecurity Research Resources at the University of the German Armed Forces, the military has now made a significant contribution to cybersecurity policy. The revised national defence strategy from 2016, so-called White Paper, provided the framework for the Bundeswehr's cyber command (Federal Government 2016). The 2016 White Paper, for the first time, takes security in the global cyber and information space as a whole into account. The document outlines the Bundeswehr's contribution to the protection of this space, as well as its operational capability in cyber and information space.

The attack on the networks of the German Bundestag in summer 2015 led to an opening of cybersecurity policy debate to the public. Via an advanced persistent threat (APT) campaign, allegedly Russian intelligence services stole a tremendous amount of data from the parliament's networks. This cyber attack against the heart of the German democratic institutions led to a major change of thinking about cyber-security. In addition to a technically-oriented cybersecurity policy focusing on data protection aspects and preventive technology management, the policy domain developed a military component and an increasingly intense discussion of active cyber defence actions.

2.5   Advantages and Disadvantages of the German Approach—A Preliminary Balance

Germany has developed the core of its cybersecurity policy along three strong lines: a rather engineering-motivated preventive and technology-oriented policy, a policy of protecting personal data motivated by high esteem for privacy through legal, technical and organisational measures and, last but not least, a policy formulated along extended criminal offences and the need to strengthen the security authority investigative powers against cyber crime. These three cornerstones have one point in common: they are primarily preventive and deeply civiliani. They are based on the idea of the ability to create cybersecurity through appropriate structuring of information technology systems, legal protection of people against misuse of these systems and the consistent prosecution of violations of the law.

Germany has made great progress with this approach. The legal foundations for the protection of IT critical infrastructures and digital services are an exemplary one, the Federal Office for Information Security is one of the largest and best-in-class cybersecurity authorities in the world. Since the first cybersecurity strategy in 2005, government and businesses have invested heavily in preventive cybersecurity. Cybersecurity in Germany has a solid legal and organisational foundation.

However, this approach has not yet been able to fully grasp the complexity of international cybersecurity. In regard to the unsolved basic security of information technology systems and the increase in complexity and vulnerabilities, Germany's technical and organisational measures cannot adequately protect companies and authorities. A purely defensive and preventive strategy does not help in this context. At the same time, the Snowden revelations and the subsequent efforts towards technological sovereignty, which have not been very successful so far, have shown that considerable shortcomings already exist at the level of technical security.

Finally, the increase in cyber attacks as part of a worldwide asymmetric threat situation has also made it clear to Germany, as a technology-supported export nation, that cybersecurity necessarily includes active, military and civilian cyber defence and that capacities must be built for this purpose.

References

Ammann T (1989) Hacker für Moskau. Deutsche Computer-Spione im Dienst des KGB. Wunder-lich, Reinbek

Bäcker M (2014) Erhebung, Bevorratung und Übermittlung von Telekommunikations-daten durch die Nachrichtendienste des Bundes. Stellungnahme zur Anhörung des NSA-Untersuchungsausschusses

Bitkom e. V. (2015) Digitale Souveränität - Positionsbestimmung und erste Handlungsempfehlungen für Deutschland und Europa, Berlin

Bundesministerium des Innern (2004) Nach dem 11. September 2001. Maßnahmen gegen den Terror, Berlin

Bundesministerium des Innern (2005) Nationaler Plan zum Schutz der Informationsinfrastrukturen (NPSI), Berlin

Bundesministerium des Innern (2011) Cyber-Sicherheitsstrategie für Deutschland, Berlin

Bundesministerium des Innern und Bundesministerium für Wirtschaft und Energie (2013) Maß-nahmen für einen besseren Schutz der Privatsphäre. Fortschrittsbericht vom 14. August 2013, 14 Aug 2013. Available: https://www.bmi.bund.de/SharedDocs/downloads/DE/veroeffentlichunge n/2013/bericht2.pdf. Accessed 03 Mar 2018

Bundesministerium des Innern, "Pressemitteilung 'Schutz der Privatsphäre durch ver-trauenswürdige Informations- und Kommunikationstechnik'," 09 Sept 2013. Available: https://www.bmi.bund.de/SharedDocs/pressemitteilungen/DE/2013/09/runder_tisch.html. Accessed 03 Mar 2018

Bundesministerium für Wirtschaft und Energie (1999) Das Jahr-2000-Problem in der Information-stechnik. Zweiter Fortschrittsbericht der Bundesregierung, Berlin

Bundesregierung (2014) Digitale Agenda für Deutschland

Bundesverfassungsgericht (2008) NJW, p 822

CDU, CSU and SPD (2013) Deutschlands Zukunft gestalten. Koalitionsvertrag für die 18. Legis-laturperiode, Berlin

Deutsche Welle (2008) New privacy scandal comes calling at Telekom, 11 Oct 2008. Available: http://www.dw.com/en/new-privacy-scandal-comes-calling-at-telekom/a-3706182. Accessed 03 Mar 2018

Deutscher Bundestag (2017) Abschlussbericht des 1. Untersuchungsausschusses (NSA) vom Juni 2017, Drucksache 18/12850, Berlin

Deutscher Bundestag (2000) Plenarprotokoll 14/102 vom 11. Mai 2000

Eckert C (2013) Digitale Vision für Europa. FAZ.NET, 23 Nov 2013

Encyclopedia Britannica (2018) Y2K Bug, 21 Feb 2018. Available: https://www.britannica.com/te chnology/Y2K-bug. Accessed 31 Mar 2018

Federal Government (2016) White Paper on German Security Policy and the Future of the Bun-deswehr, Berlin

Funke M (2013) Bundeskabinett: Fortschrittsbericht zum besseren Schutz der Privatsphäre. CR, p R94

GDPR EU (2016) Regulation 2016/679 of the European Parliament and of the Council of 27 April 2016 on the protection of natural persons with regard to the processing of personal data and on the free movement of such data, and repealing Directive 95/46/EC, OJ L, no 119, p 1

Gellman B, Poitras L (2013) U.S., British intelligence mining data from nine U.S. Internet companies in broad secret programme, Washington Post, 07 June 2013. Available: https://www. washingtonpost.com/investigations/us-intelligence-mining-data-from-nine-us-internet-compani es-in-broad-secret-programme/2013/06/06/3a0c0da8-cebf-11e2-8845-d970ccb04497_story.htm l?noredirect=on&utm_term=.7019ae7824f8. Accessed 31 Mar 2018

Gesetz zum Schutz vor Mißbrauch personenbezogener Daten bei der Datenverarbeitung as of January 27, 1977, published on February 1, 1977. Entry into force since January 1, 1978, BGBl. I, no 7, p 201

Gesetz zur Erhöhung der Sicherheit informationstechnischer Systeme (IT-Sicherheitsgesetz) vom 17. Juli 2015, BGBl. I, p 1324

Hathaway ME (2014) Connected choices: how the internet is challenging sovereign decisions. Am Foreign Policy Interests 36(5):300–313

Hornung G (2008) Ein neues Grundrecht. Kommentierung zur BVerfG-Entscheidung. CR, p 299

Lauer C, Lobo S (2015) Aufstieg und Niedergang der Piratenpartei, Hamburg: sobooks.de

Lenckner T, Winkelbauer, W (1986) Computerkriminalität - Möglichkeiten und Grenzen des 2. WiKG, CR, pp 483–488

Michaelis P (2016) Der "Stand der Technik" im Kontext regulatorischer Anforderungen. DuD, p 45

NIS Directive EU (2016) Directive 2016/1148 of the European Parliament and of the Council of 6 July 2016 concerning measures for a high common level of security of network and information systems across the Union. OJ L, no 194, p 1

Oppliger R (1992) Computersicherheit. Eine Einführung, Braunschweig, Wiesbaden

Rosenbach M, Stark H (2014) Der NSA-Komplex. Edward Snowden und der Weg in die totale Überwachung. DVA, München

Schaar P (2015) Globale Überwachung und digitale Souveränität. Zeitschrift für Außen- und Sicherheitspolitik 8:447–459

Schallbruch M, Gaycken S, Skierka I (2018) Cybersicherheit 2018–2020: Handlungsvorschläge für CDU/CSU und SPD. DSI Industry & Policy Recommendations (IPR) Series, no 1

Schreibauer M, Hessel TJ (2007) Das 41. Strafrechtsänderungsgesetz zur Bekämpfung der Computerkriminalität, K&R, pp 616–620

Schulze T (2006) Bedingt abwehrbereit. Schutz kritischer Informations-Infrastrukturen in Deutschland und den USA. VS Verlag, Wiesbaden

Stoll C (1989) The cuckoo's egg, New York

Wetzling T (2016) The key to intelligence reform in Germany: strengthening the G 10-commission's role to authorise strategic surveillance. Stiftung Neue Verantwortung, Berlin

Chapter 3
The Evolution of German Cybersecurity Strategy

Abstract This chapter traces the evolution of German cybersecurity strategy throughout the past two and a half decades. During this period, the German approach to cybersecurity strategy has developed from a civilian preventive one to a more comprehensive one, which today includes strategic military aspects. In following, this chapter illustrates the development of cybersecurity strategy in three phases. The first phase (1991 to 2011) marks the emergence of cybersecurity as a strategic issue in the context of critical information infrastructure protection. In the second phase (2011 to 2016), the government consolidated existing policies after adopting its first national cybersecurity strategy in 2011. The Snowden revelations in 2013 lifted cybersecurity sharply up the political agenda. In the third phase, from 2016 to early 2018, Germany adopted its second national cybersecurity strategy that outlines a comprehensive approach to cybersecurity, as well as a national defence strategy, which for the first time emphasised the strategic military dimension of cybersecurity within a hybrid warfare context. In 2017 and 2018, intensified discussions about the offensive aspects of government hacking indicated a further turn in toward a more expansive cybersecurity policy.

Keywords Cybersecurity strategy · Critical infrastructure protection
IT security law · Snowden · White paper on security policy

3.1 Introduction

Once a niche topic in German politics, cybersecurity has become a strategic national policy issue. At the time of writing, Germany has adopted three national cybersecurity-related strategies: The National Plan for the Protection of Information Infrastructures in 2005, the first Cybersecurity Strategy for Germany in 2011, and the second Cybersecurity Strategy for Germany in 2016.

Since the emergence of the first efforts to improve IT security at the national level, cybersecurity strategy in Germany has followed a technical and preventive approach, which focuses on the protection of IT systems and the civil defence of critical (infor-

© The Author(s) 2018
M. Schallbruch and I. Skierka, *Cybersecurity in Germany*, SpringerBriefs
in Cybersecurity, https://doi.org/10.1007/978-3-319-90014-8_3

mation) infrastructures. To this date, the protection of critical infrastructures (CIs) remains an essential part of German strategic efforts in the field of cybersecurity. Besides, the enhancement of counter cyber crime and espionage capabilities, as well as human resources and research and education are vital issues emphasised throughout all German national cybersecurity strategies (NCSSs). More recently, the government began to promote the strategic and military dimensions of cybersecurity, as well as the deployment of offensive use of IT, within the 2016 cybersecurity strategy, the 2016 national defence strategy, and the 2018 coalition government treaty.

Overall, German cybersecurity policy and strategy developments are situated in an environment shaped by a changing information security threat landscape, domestic political processes, (cyber) policy developments in other states (Cavelty 2014, p. 10), and "focusing events" (Kingdon 2003), such as the Snowden revelations.

Developments in cybersecurity strategy and policy occur in five dimensions, which the analysis will continuously take into account. These dimensions each have their own emphasis and discourse followed by different government departments (Cavelty 2014, Hathaway and Klimburg 2012):

- Technical cybersecurity: referring to the protection of computing and communication technologies from unauthorized access or attack by malware and system intrusion.
- Critical infrastructure protection and national crisis management: relating to preventive and reactive approaches to protect critical infrastructures and society as a whole from technically induced accidents, physical, and cyber attacks.
- Counter cyber crime and espionage: referring to security efforts which enable the protection of information from businesses, governments, and individuals from theft, manipulation, or sabotage by criminals or nation state actors.
- Military: referring to cyber activities encompassing the protection of the armed forces' networks, as well as the enabling of the state's own network centric warfare capabilities and strategic cyber warfare.
- International diplomatic dimension: referring to the diplomatic negotiations and efforts by governments to keep the digital realm safe and secure from threats and inter-state conflict.

3.2 Phase 1, 1991–2011: IT Security and Critical Infrastructure Protection

As the previous chapter outlined, cybersecurity policy was strongly linked to data protection and technical or organizational aspects of IT security for many years. Germany's efforts to address IT security in a systematic manner at the federal level began shortly after German reunification in late 1990, when it adopted the law establishing the Federal Office for Information Security (Bundesamt für Sicherheit in der Informationstechnik, BSI) (BSI 1990). With the entering into force of the law in 1991, the BSI emerged as the successor of a German foreign intelligence service's

(Bundesnachrichtendienst, BND) sub-office which had been responsible for tech-nologically protecting government secrets. The newly established BSI obtained the mandate to coordinate IT security efforts among government, industry, and society in Germany and would remain at the centre of most subsequent cybersecurity policy developments (see Chap. 4).

Throughout the 1990s, public awareness for "new" asymmetric and borderless security threats, such as international crime and terrorism, as well as for the vul-nerability of societies' infrastructures grew. It became clear that modern societies were dependent on essential infrastructures that increasingly relied on inherently insecure IT-systems, and thereby posed "soft targets" for criminal or terrorist adver-saries (Brunner and Suter 2008). The disruption of vital infrastructures in sectors such as information and telecommunications, energy, water, banking and finance, and others, could trigger a national security crisis. Per the official German definition, critical infrastructures (CI) are "organizational and physical structures and facili-ties of such vital importance to a nation's society and economy that their failure or degradation would result in sustained supply shortages, significant disruption of public safety and security, or other dramatic consequences" (Federal Ministry of the Interior 2009, p. 4).

The United States (US) was the first country to adopt CI protection (CIP) policies In 1996, President Bill Clinton set up the US President's Commission on Critical Infrastructure Protection (PCCIP). In 1997, the commission issued a report that con-cluded the US needed to see CIP through a national security lens and take preventive measures, with a focus on information security (President's Commission on Critical Infrastructure Protection 1997). Motivated by the US PCCIP, the German Federal Ministry of the Interior (BMI) initiated an inter-ministerial working group on CIs (AG KRITIS[1]) in 1997 (Schulze 2006, p. 155). The working group comprised ministerial representatives, a steering committee, and a permanent office at the BSI. Its mandate was to describe possible threat scenarios for German CIs, conduct a vulnerability analysis of Germany's crucial sectors, suggest countermeasures, and delineate an early-warning system (Petermann 2011). In its (unpublished) 1999 report, the group concluded that IT security and the protection of CIs would have high relevance for German national safety and economic well-being in the future (Kurzbericht der Ressortarbeitsgruppe KRITIS 1999).[2] The terrorist attacks from 11 September 2001 raised additional awareness for threats to CIs and added urgency to ongoing efforts. Moreover, they led to intensified international cooperation in the area of CIP, for example within NATO, the OECD and the G8 (Schulze 2006, p. 267).

After a number of internal sectoral CI studies conducted by the BSI (Brunner and Suter 2008), the government finally presented a National Plan for Information Infrastructure Protection (NPSI) in 2005 (Bundesministerium des Innern 2005a), as well as a Baseline Protection Concept for the physical protection of CIs (Bundesmin-

---

[1] The abbreviation KRITIS is an official abbreviation for "kritische Infrastrukturen" meaning "crit-ical infrastructures".

[2] A late draft version (7.95) of the report leaked and is accessible online via (Kurzbericht der Ressortarbeitsgruppe KRITIS - Entwurfsversion and Dec 1999).

isterium des Innern 2005b). The focus of the NPSI were information infrastructures, which it defines as "the entirety of the IT components of an infrastructure" (Bundesministerium des Innern 2005a). Since most CIs are increasingly digitised and interconnected, critical information infrastructures (CIIs) are an essential part of CIs. The very distinction between CIs and CIIs can seldom be made anymore today.

The NPSI is the first IT security-related national strategy in Germany. It directly links information infrastructures to national security, mentioning "new" threats such as the deployment of malware for criminal or terrorist ends, which could lead to an outage of vital information infrastructures. Overall, it is a preventive plan. It focuses on measures to strengthen IT security of the nation's IT-dependent infrastructures along three strategic objectives:

- Prevention—adequately protecting information infrastructures
- Preparedness—responding effectively to IT security incidents
- Sustainability—enhancing German competence in IT security and setting international standards.

The implementation of corresponding measures, according to the strategy, is the shared responsibility of the government, critical infrastructure operators in particular, and society as a whole. In this spirit, the NPSI announces two CIP implementation plans—a mandatory one for the federal administration ("UP Bund" or "implementation plan Bund"), and a public-private one for critical infrastructures ("UP KRITIS" or "implementation plan for critical infrastructure protection (CIP)"). The respective implementation plans entered into force in 2007 (see Chap. 4).

Moreover, the NPSI defined the newly established "IT crisis response centre" as a national command, control, and analysis centre, which has become an integral part of national crisis management (see Chap. 4). Under the strategic objective "sustainability," the NPSI established the goal to promote the development of trusted German IT products and services, particularly the encryption industry—a theme that would reappear in many following policies. Regarding the international dimension, the strategy advocates intensified cooperation with European and international partners in the field of CIP and emphasises that the government will advocate its interests in international organizations and standard-setting bodies. In the 2000s, Germany did indeed actively participate in efforts at bringing forward the European Programme for Critical Infrastructure Protection (COM 2006), which led to the Directive on European Critical Infrastructures in 2008, and contributed to the EU Network Information Security Directive in 2016.

Following the establishment of the CIP implementation plans in 2007, the government adopted its first comprehensive strategy for the protection of critical infrastructures (CIP strategy) in 2009 (Federal Ministry of the Interior 2009). The CIP has a wider focus than the NPSI in that it focuses on all CIs, not only information infrastructures. It defines nine CI sectors, which it divides into "technical basic infrastructures" and "socio-economic service infrastructures" (Federal Ministry of the Interior 2009, p. 7):

Technical basic infrastructures	Socio-economic service infrastructures
Power supply	Public health; Food
Information and communication technologies	Emergency and rescue services, disaster control and management
Transportation	Parliament, government, public administration, law enforcement agencies
(Drinking-) water supply and sewage disposal	Finance, insurance business
	Media, cultural objects (including cultural heritage objects)

The strategy emphasises the interdependencies between the different infrastructures and cascading risks resulting from potential outages. For example, a
power outage would affect multiple socio-economic service infrastructures, and the
breakdown of public administration and government would significantly affect the
functioning of technical basic infrastructures. It re-emphasises the shared responsibility between the federal government, state (Länder) and municipal authorities,
CI operators, and industry, and outlines prevention, response, and sustainability
mechanisms. It announces the establishment of security partnership platforms at all
government levels and emphasises the need for international cooperation, especially
at the European level.

Overall, the NPSI laid the groundwork for subsequent cybersecurity policies and
the NCSS in 2011. The protection of CIs would remain a core strategic objective of
all cybersecurity efforts to come. Together with the more comprehensive 2009 CIP
strategy, it formed an integral part of future CIP policies specifically, including an
updated CIP implementation plan and council in 2014, and the 2015 IT security law.
The plan's goal to promote "trusted German IT" would remain a leitmotiv within
German cybersecurity strategy and gain greater traction again in the wake of the
Snowden revelations. Other goals related to effective cyber prevention and defence,
the enhancement of BSI's functions and competencies, and a prioritization of IT
security in education, training, and research and development, would equally be
taken up by following strategies.

Moreover, the NPSI outlined a "whole of nation" approach, which emphasises
the shared responsibility for IT security among the government, operators of critical
infrastructures, private companies, and individuals. In a fast evolving area like digital
policy, the rationale behind a whole of nation approach is that "specific 'cooperation' is needed from such a great number of non-state actors that a pure legislative
approach would be largely unworkable in most democracies" (Hathaway and Klimburg 2012, p. 31). To this date, cooperation among stakeholders is a building block of
German cybersecurity policy. However, that cooperation has long focused on civilian
government actors, with the role of military forces being marginal, and on industry
on the non-state actor side, leaving out civil society stakeholders until the second
NCSS in 2016.

3.3   Phase 2: 2011–2016: Building a Civilian Cybersecurity Strategy

3.3.1   The First National Cybersecurity Strategy for Germany

In 2011, the federal German government adopted its first national cybersecurity strategy (NCSS) (Bundesministerium des Innern 2011). The strategy is an advancement of the 2005 NPSI and the CIP implementation plan (Kullik 2014, p. 92).

The NCSS widens the scope of cybersecurity policy from a somewhat technical infrastructure-specific to a societal strategic issue, which includes the economic, social, and cultural interactions taking place in the digital realm (Bundesministerium des Innern 2011). It has an explicitly civilian focus, which can be complemented by the Armed Forces' (Bundeswehr's) protection measures of their capabilities as well as other measures to make cybersecurity "a part of Germany's preventive security strategy." Like the NPSI, an overall guiding principle of the NCSS is the whole of nation approach emphasising that public and private stakeholders have to act as partners and fulfill protection tasks together (Bundesministerium des Innern 2011, p. 4).

Cybersecurity according to the NCSS is "the desired objective of the IT security situation, in which the risk of (global) cyberspace has been reduced to an acceptable minimum." This definition applies to civilian as well as military IT systems. Cyberspace, per the strategy's definition, is "the virtual space of all IT systems linked at data level on a global scale." Hence, non-internet connected IT systems are not considered part of cyberspace (Bundesministerium des Innern 2011, p. 14).

The NCSS's stated vision is to make a substantial contribution to a secure cyberspace, thus "maintaining and promoting economic and social prosperity in Germany" (Bundesministerium des Innern 2011, p. 4). A national strategy would ideally translate that vision into a national action plan, a set of strategic objectives to achieve it, and guidelines on how such resources are to be applied to reach stated objectives (Luiijf et al. 2013, p. 4). However, the document falls short of providing a clear guide of action to achieve specific strategic objectives. As Luiijf et al. (2013, p. 13) note in their comparative analysis of the NCSS of nineteen nations, the German NCSS presents a set of strategic priority areas which other NCSS present as action lines. Indeed, the document itself refers to the ten points it outlines as "objectives and measures":

1.   Protection of critical information infrastructures
2.   Secure IT systems in Germany
3.   Strengthening IT security in the public administration
4.   National Cyber Response Centre
5.   National Cybersecurity Council
6.   Effective crime control also in cyberspace

7.   Effective coordinated action to ensure cybersecurity in Europe and worldwide
8.   Use of reliable and trustworthy information technology
9.   Personnel development in federal authorities
10.   Tools to respond to cyber attacks.

Among these objectives and measures, the protection of CIs has been most successfully implemented by the 2015 IT security law (see 3.3.2). The measures outlined in 2., 3., 4., and 5. contribute to this strategic objective. The enhancement of secure IT systems (2.) is a recurring topic in German cybersecurity policy. Its implementation has been partially successful. As announced under the action line, the BSI has intensified its information and awareness efforts on IT security risks, and the state has provided incentives for essential security functions certified by the state, such as electronic identity proof or De-Mail. However, uptake remains very low in practice (eGovernment Monitor 2017). The related goal to "strengthen Germany's technological sovereignty and economic capacity" through intensified incentivization of research and development in IT security has to date not yielded any tangible results, although this agenda has been vigorously promoted after the Snowden revelations (see Chap. 1 and 5). Hence, the development of secure IT in Germany and Europe remains an ongoing issue.

While the government did establish a national cyber response centre and a national cybersecurity council, the former has not been a success (see Chap. 4). An overarching effective national cybersecurity architecture with cross-institutional cooperation mechanisms is still lacking. The related goal to develop a set of comprehensive sustainable tools to respond to cyber attacks (10.) remains very vague in the strategy. Indeed, points like this one which does not contain any concrete propositions point to the overall weakness of the strategy document, namely its lack of an outline of strategic objectives, resources, and means with which to achieve those, and ways in which to use these resources.

The lack of qualified personnel to implement the federal government's cybersecurity policies has become one of the biggest challenges in cybersecurity policy today (Schuetze 2018)—hence, personnel development in federal authorities (9.) is still highly relevant.

The NCSS highlights the growing importance of international cooperation for the improvement of cybersecurity for the fight against cyber crime (6.) and the prevention of inter-state conflict (7.). Germany has been a signatory of the Council of Europe's Budapest Convention on Cybercrime since 2001. Bilateral and multilateral cooperation among law enforcement agencies and with the private sector remain ongoing challenges, which Germany continues to address via national public-private partnerships and collaboration with international partners, including through the European Centre for Cyber Crime. With its reference to coordinated action at the EU and international levels (7.), the NCSS for the first time strategically outlines the international fora and organizations in which Germany should be active diplomatically. Due to the borderless nature of cyberspace and uncertain spillover effects of cybersecurity risks, its promotion of international norms is an essential and ongoing priority. Hence, the strategy underlines the enforcement of international rules of conduct, standards, and norms as one of the guiding principles for the attainment of cybersecurity goals. Germany had indeed been active in the United Nations Group of Governmental Experts (UN GGE) to negotiate norms of responsible state behavior in cyberspace since its inception in 2004. In this context, the NCSS links to the EU's Digital Agenda and promotes the establishment of "a code for state conduct in cyberspace (cyber code)" at the international level, which should be signed by as many countries as possible, and which shall include confidence-building measures.

3.3.2 The IT Security Law

As mentioned above, the protection of CIIs is among the most successfully implemented objectives of the first NCSS. The 2013 government coalition treaty outlining the ruling parties CDU/CSU and SPD's political agenda included the proposition to adopt an "IT security law" that should build on previous efforts to improve critical infrastructure protection through regulation of operators of critical infrastructures. In June 2015, the government implemented this proposition and adopted one of the first laws regulating the IT security of CIs in Europe. Discussions about IT security mechanisms for CI operators had already been ongoing at the European level for a while, and the equivalent European Network and Information Security (NIS) directive followed only one year later, in 2016. The German IT security law is, in fact, a legislative act amending the existing law establishing the BSI. It entered into force in July 2015 and is a direct continuation and a vital consolidation of previous efforts to improve CI security. Since an ever-growing share of society and its CIs rely on inherently insecure digital technologies, related cybersecurity risks increased.

Therefore, the law imposes several obligations on the operators of critical infrastructures in seven sectors (energy, health, information and telecommunication technologies, transportation, water, food, and the finance and insurance sectors). Government and public administration as well as media and culture are classified as critical infrastructures, but already regulated by other legislative acts and therefore not included into the IT security law. The law creates mandatory reporting requirements, under which CI operators need to report potential and actual significant IT security incidents to the BSI. Besides the BSI, the BKA will have a role in investigating cyberattacks against CIs in this context. Such reporting requirements had already been suggested by the EU in 2013 (Bendiek 2013). Decision-making in the German and other European governments saw incident information sharing as a necessary measure to ensure adequate CIP. Voluntary information sharing mechanisms had only been partially effective. CI operators and other private companies do not have a natural incentive to share incident information, which can result in reputational and financial loss as well as in potential liability claims. This is why policy-makers pushed for the institutionalization of incident information sharing (Zedler 2016, p. 39).

Moreover, CI operators need to implement mandatory minimum IT security standards which correspond to the "technical state of the art." The respective operators within their sectors determine that "state of the art". After an elaborate coordination process between sectoral industry associations and governmental experts, the Ministry of Interior issued two regulations which further specify which critical services will be affected by the law regarding specific threshold values. The Ministry issued the respective regulations in May 2016 for the energy, water, food, and ICT sectors, and in 2017 for the health, finance and insurance, transportation, and logistics sectors. The services identified in the regulations have to implement the necessary standards and legal requirements within two years until mid-2018 and mid-2019, respectively.

3.3.3   The Snowden Revelations

As the previous chapter illustrated, the revelations by Edward Snowden in 2013 constitute a "focusing event" (Kingdon 2003) in German cybersecurity policy and intensified the public debate about data security, surveillance, and espionage. In the wake of the revelations, cybersecurity became a highly political matter. Counter-espionage and privacy became defining issues permeating official policies and strategic documents, such as the 2013 coalition government treaty or the German government's Digital Agenda from 2014 (Bundesregierung 2014). The once prominent calls for "technological" or "digital sovereignty" regarding enhancing control over data flows in Germany or strengthening the German IT industry never developed into a coherent strategy. Today, "digital sovereignty" is a political expression used for various measures ranging from the enhancement of data protection and informational self-determination of individual citizens to promoting the national IT industry and reducing the dependence on foreign IT components (Eckert 2013; Bitkom 2015).

An important consequence of the Snowden revelations was the establishment of a parliamentary inquiry committee investigating the NSA's data collection practices, as well as German intelligence agencies' cooperation with the NSA and other "Five Eye Alliance" intelligence services such as the British GCHQ. As mentioned in the previous chapter, the committee found that the German Foreign Intelligence Service (Bundesnachrichtendienst, BND) had closely collaborated with the NSA in monitoring international telecommunications on German territory (Rosenbach and Stark 2014; Deutscher Bundestag 2017) and thereby engaged in illegal practices, according to German constitutional law experts (Bäcker 2014; Wetzling 2016). In October 2016, the German parliament adopted a controversial law that expanded the agency's surveillance powers (BND-Gesetz 2016). On the basis of this law, the BND now has the authority to collect and process information including personal data from telecommunications networks on German territory, as long as the data stems from communications between foreigners.

3.4   Phase 3, 2016–2018: Consolidating a Comprehensive Civilian-Military Approach to Cybersecurity

In November 2016, the German federal government adopted its second NCSS. In July of the same year, the government passed its second national defence strategy, the "White Paper on German Security Policy and the future of the Bundeswehr (Armed Forces)" (Federal Government 2016). The White Paper for the first time specifically outlines strategic military aspects of cybersecurity.

3.4.1   The 2016 White Paper on German Security Policy and the Future of the Bundeswehr

The 2016 White Paper is the German Armed Forces' response to a rapidly globalizing, high-tech threat environment. It presents the response to threats emerging from the cyber and information domain as a major security policy challenge for Germany. The term "cyber" appears more than 70 times in the 139-page document. Cyber attacks, and other threats, such as epidemics and transnational terrorism, are part of new risks in a globalized world, in which internal and external boundaries become blurred.

Apart from cyber attacks that can cause physical damage, the White Paper mentions disinformation campaigns as a particular challenge for open and pluralistic societies, referring to them as "the use of digital communication to influence public opinion, for example through hidden attempts to sway discussions on social media and by manipulating information on news portals" (Federal Government 2016, p. 36). Cyber attacks and disinformation campaigns are instruments of hybrid warfare, which aims to not only militarily, but also politically destabilize the opponent and its society.

The White Paper's response to the successful prevention of hybrid threats is "whole-of-society" resilience. According to the document, resilience can only be achieved by efficiently linking relevant policy areas, including better CIP, disaster control, civil defence, and border controls, among others. International cooperation with NATO and EU allies and diplomatic measures such as confidence-building and conflict resolution mechanisms become crucial.

Concerning cyber capabilities, the White Paper declares that the defence against cyber attacks necessitates high-value defensive and offensive capacities. Following a "whole-of-government" approach, the Bundeswehr needs to cooperate with civilian actors, such as research institutions and industry, develop Bundeswehr cyber capabilities, and increase the robustness of its weapons systems. Moreover, it needs to recruit "the very best personnel by creating attractive career paths in cyber."

When the government unveiled the White Paper, the Ministry of Defence had already adopted an internal strategy that established a dedicated "cyber and information command" (CIR command) in the Bundeswehr. Chapter 4 further elaborates on the CIR command, which is operational since April 2017.

3.4.2 The 2016 Second National Cybersecurity Strategy

In November 2016, the government adopted a second, updated NCSS (Bundesminis-terium des Innern 2016). Compared to the first strategy, it outlines strategic objectives, means, and action items in a more coherent and structured way. This decisive char-acter is the result of a longer and more comprehensive drafting process, as well as an advanced stage of experience with cybersecurity among decision-makers. While policy-makers had drafted the first NCSS in a quick and somewhat un-coordinated process, the second NCSS emerged from a year-long coordination process among different ministries. The Ministry of Interior led both drafting procedures but the sec-ond one was influenced by the Ministry of Defence and the Federal Foreign Office to a much greater extent than the 2011 strategy.

It outlines four areas of action:

– Safe and Self-determined Action in a Digitised Environment

This first area of action adopts a user-centric perspective to cybersecurity. Most other strategies and policies had not focused on the specific needs of individual users, but rather on society as a whole. The NCSS promotes the enhancement of digital literacy, awareness raising, secure e-identities, as well as strengthened certification and approval of ICTs and the introduction of an IT security "quality label." Such a label should make it easier for consumers and small and medium-sized enterprises to assess the security of IT products and thereby strengthen trust in IT.

The section also outlines how digital innovation across society can be designed securely. Accordingly, new policies, for example in the areas of e-health or mobility, should take into account both the economic benefits of new digital business models as well as the security of society and consumers. It advocates an evaluation of respon-sibilities and liability laws for vulnerable software. Moreover, the section promotes IT security by design.

As a final cross-cutting issue, the section announces new investments in various research and development initiatives and clusters. Here, the strategy can point to several existing successful research initiatives, which shows that the government has continuously invested in research and development initiatives in the field of IT.

– A Joint Effort of Government and Industry

In this area, the strategy emphasises the continued need for trusted public-private cooperation and again takes up the cooperative "whole of nation" approach already advocated in previous strategies. This action area focuses on CIP, referring to the IT security law and the CIP implementation plan, and the enhancement of counter cyber crime and espionage measures to protect German companies. It also advocates industrial policy measures to strengthen the German IT industry. The term "tech-nological sovereignty" is notably absent from this section, but it outlines goals to promote better the development of key technologies and quality IT "made in Ger-many." The NCSS further proposes measures to improve cooperation with providers in the defence against cyber attacks, for example IoT botnets. Indeed, the government has passed corresponding measures within the adoption of the EU NIS Directive implementation law in May 2017, which has extended the legal basis for Internet providers to conduct "light packet inspection" and conduct sinkholing and network blockage (Schallbruch 2017).

– An Effective and Sustainable Cybersecurity Architecture

In this section, the strategy addresses some shortcomings in the national cybersecurity architecture and proposes measures for better coordination and the enhancement of cyber defence effectiveness (see Chap. 4). It announces the further development of the national cyber response centre established in 2011 and the strengthening of on-site analysis and response capacities through so-called "Mobile Incident Response Teams" (MIRTs). It also aims to strengthen CERT structures in Germany, to better protect the federal administration, and to strengthen cooperation between federal and state level authorities for cybersecurity.

One of the section's most essential propositions is the goal to gain and develop more IT security personnel and efficiently using available resources. However, the strategy misses mentioning any concrete numbers or metrics, which leaves the proposition vague.

The NCSS also announces to intensify law enforcement activities in cyberspace through the deployment of new data analysis and forensic technologies, as well as better personnel resources. Furthermore, it announces measures to better fight cyber espionage and sabotage, including the strengthening of the domestic intelligence service's (Bundesverfassungsschutz) capabilities and an early-warning system for the foreign intelligence service BND. In addition, the section announces the establishment of a central office for IT in the security sphere (ZITiS), which will develop cyber capabilities, including hacking tools, for police agencies and domestic intelligence services. Another novel aspect in this section is the explicit reference to the military dimension of cybersecurity and the Armed Forces' 2016 White Paper.

The announcement of these capabilities has been controversially discussed. For the first time, an NCSS transparently outlines offensive capability development schemes for intelligence and police agencies. This development constitutes a departure from earlier strategies and policies, which exclusively emphasised the state's defensive capabilities and approaches.

In comparison to cybersecurity strategies and policies of other nations, however, this is not unusual. The US, France or the UK, for example, had already long endorsed offensive and defensive capabilities within their comprehensive NCSS. The growing number, complexity, and sophistication of cyber threats further contribute to the necessity of nations to outline responses, including offensive capabilities.

– The Active Positioning of Germany in European and International Cybersecurity
  Policy Discussions

In this NCSS, the international diplomatic dimension of cybersecurity has finally become a key strategic priority. The government proclaims that it aims to actively shape an effective European cybersecurity policy, to further advance the NATO cyber defence policy, and to actively participate in shaping cybersecurity internationally, including norms for responsible state behavior and confidence-building measures in the UN or the OSCE.

Germany has long been an active part of the UN GGE negotiations. In 2015, the German Foreign Ministry led a new round of those negotiations on responsible norms for state behavior. Unfortunately, the negotiations ended without consensus, and for now, the process is on halt at the UN level. It would be in Germany's best interest to (re-)initiate new norms or confidence-building processes at the international level (see Chap. 5).

With its goal to engage in global cyber capacity building efforts, the strategy does not only promote a foreign policy, but also a development policy goal. This point underlines the importance of strengthening cybersecurity internationally in the face of borderless threats. Finally, as in previous strategies, Germany plans to enhance international cooperation in the fight against cyber crime.

3.4.3   Taking Stock of Past Developments for Future Cybersecurity Strategies

Since 2005, the German government has successively expanded its cybersecurity strategy. The latest NCSS covers almost all relevant fields of action. Nevertheless, German cybersecurity policy lacks distinct strategic cornerstones and clear priorities. A national strategy should ideally identify strategic objectives ("ends"), pinpoint the resources available to reach those objectives ("means"), and provide a guide to how such resources are to be applied to reach stated objectives ("ways") (Lindstrom and Luiijf 2012). While the 2016 NCSS has a broader scope than the first NCSS from 2011, it constitutes a work program for respective federal government agencies rather than a strategic program for Germany. It outlines objectives and action lines but does not delineate clear responsibilities and does not allocate measurable resources for the implementation of the goals. Moreover, it lacks concrete measurable goals against which achievements can be evaluated.

The 2018 coalition government treaty outlines several fields of action for the government, which mainly complement existing lines of action in the area of research and development and the enhancement of the security of IT products (CDU/CSU and SPD 2018). It outlines the government's plans to expand the existing IT security law to an "IT security law 2.0", which shall increase the responsibilities of manufacturers and providers of IT products beyond the area of critical infrastructures. It promises to enhance research and development in the field of IT security, to set up competence centres, and to make secure electronic identification and end-to-end encryption solutions more easily accessible to citizens. Besides, it aims to develop minimum IT security standards for internet connected products in cooperation with industry and introduce a quality label indicating the security level of IT products for consumers.

On the institutional side, it aims to strengthen the BSI's role in cybersecurity and to create a new cyber alliance with industry to enhance trusted cooperation between industry and public authorities.

Hence, the coalition treaty presents a range of necessary IT security measures that have the potential to increase the level of technical protection of IT in Germany. However, it almost entirely omits political questions of cybersecurity. These issues include the debated government's expansion of offensive capabilities for government hacking purposes and discussions about active cyber defence under the umbrella term "hack backs." This leaves a number of strategic questions unanswered, which Chap. 5 will discuss in more detail.

References

BSI-Errichtungsgesetz vom 17. Dezember 1990 (BGBl. I S. 2834), zuletzt geändert durch Artikel 11 der Verordnung vom 25. November 2003 (BGBl. I S. 2304) (1990)
Bendiek A (2013) Kritische Infrastrukturen, Cybersicherheit, Datenschutz. Die EU schlägt Pflöcke für digitale Standortpolitik ein. Stiftung für Wissenschaft und Politik, Berlin
Bitkom e.V (2015) Digitale Souveränität - Positionsbestimmung und erste Handlungsempfehlungen für Deutschland und Europa, Berlin
Brunner EM, Suter M (2008) International CIIP handbook 2008/2009. Center for Security Studies Zurich, Zurich
BND-Gesetz (2016) Gesetz zur Ausland-Ausland-Fernmeldeaufklärung des Bundesnachrichten-dienstes vom 30 Dec 2016, Bundesgesetzblatt Teil I, p. 3346
Bundesministerium des Innern (2005a) Nationaler Plan zum Schutz der Informationsinfrastrukturen (NPSI), Berlin
Bundesministerium des Innern (2005b) Schutz Kritsicher Infrastrukturen - Basisschutzkonzept, Berlin
Bundesministerium des Innern (2011) Cyber-Sicherheitsstrategie für Deutschland, Berlin
Bundesministerium des Innern (2016) Cyber-Sicherheitsstrategie für Deutschland, Berlin
Bundesregierung (2014) Digitale Agenda für Deutschland
Bäcker M (2014) Erhebung, Bevorratung und Übermittlung von Telekommunikations-daten durch die Nachrichtendienste des Bundes. Stellungnahme zur Anhörung des NSA-Untersuchungsausschusses
CDU/CSU and SPD (2018) Ein neuer Aufbruch für Europa. Eine neue Dynamik für Deutschland. Ein neuer Zusammenhalt für unser Land. Koalitionsvertrag zwischen CDU/CSU und SPD, 19. Legislaturperiode, Berlin
COM (2006) 786 final—Communication from the Commission on a European Programme for Critical Infrastructure Protection. Commission of the European Communities, Brussels
Cavelty MD (2014) Cybersecurity in Switzerland. Springer, Heidelberg and Berlin
Cavelty MD, Suter M (2012) The art of CIIP strategy: Tacking stock of content and processes. Critical Information Infrastructure Protection, Berlin, Heidelberg, Springer-Verlag, pp 15-38
Deutscher Bundestag (2017) Abschlussbericht des 1. Untersuchungsausschusses (NSA) vom Juni 2017, Drucksache 18/12850, Berlin
Eckert C (2013) Digitale Vision für Europa. FAZ.NET, 23 Nov 2013
eGovernment Monitor 2017, Initiative D21, 2017
Federal Government (2016) White paper on german security policy and the future of the Bundeswehr, Berlin

Federal Ministry of the Interior (2009) National Strategy for Critical infrastructure Protection. Available: https://www.bmi.bund.de/SharedDocs/downloads/EN/publikationen/2009/kritis_eng lisch.html. Accessed 20 Jun 2018

Hathaway M, Klimburg A (2012) "Preliminary Considerations: On National Cyber Security. In: National cyber security framework manual. NATO Cooperative Cyber Defence Centre of Excellence, Tallinn, pp 1–43

Kingdon JW (2003) Agendas, alternatives, and public policies. Harper Collins College Publishers, New York

Kullik J (2014) Vernetzte (Un-)Sicherheit? Eine politisch-rechtliche Analyse der deutschen Cybersicherheitspolitik. Kovač, Hamburg

Kurzbericht der Ressortarbeitsgruppe KRITIS - Entwurfsversion 7.95, 03 Dec 1999. Available: http://userpage.fu-berlin.de/~bendrath/Kritis-12-1999.html. Accessed 20 Jun 2018

Lindstrom G, Luiijf E (2012) Political aims and policy methods. National cybersecurity framework manual. NATO CCDCOE, Tallinn, pp 44–65

Luiijf E, Besseling K, de Graaf P (2013) Nineteen national cyber security strategies. Int J Crit Infrastruct Prot 9(1–2):3–31

Petermann T (2011) Was bei einem Blackout geschieht: Folgen eines langandauernden und großflächigen Stromausfalls, edition sigma

President's Commission on Critical Infrastructure Protection (1997) Critical foundations. Protecting America's infrastructures. US Government Printing Office, Washington DC

Rosenbach M, Stark H (2014) Der NSA-Komplex. Edward Snowden und der Weg in die totale Überwachung, DVA, München

Schallbruch M (2017) IT-Sicherheit: Bundestag verabschiedet NIS-Umsetzungsgesetz, 14 May 2017. Available: https://www.cr-online.de/blog/2017/05/14/it-sicherheit-bundestag-verabschied et-nis-umsetzungsgesetz/. Accessed 20 Jun 2018

Schuetze J (2018) Warum dem Staat IT-Sicherheitsexpert:innen fehlen. Stiftung Neue Verantwortung, Berlin

Schulze T (2006) Bedingt abwehrbereit. Schutz kritischer Informations-Infrastrukturen in Deutschland und den USA. VS Verlag, Wiesbaden

Wetzling T (2016) The key to intelligence reform in Germany: strengthening the G 10-commission's role to authorise strategic surveillance. Stiftung Neue Verantwortung, Berlin

Zedler D (2016) Zur strategischen Planung von Cyber Security in Deutschland. Universität zu Köln, Köln, Lehrstuhl Internationale Politik

Chapter 4
The Organisation
of Cybersecurity in Germany

Abstract Cybersecurity as a responsibility of public institutions and as a field of cooperation between the government and the private sector is at odds with existing responsibilities. The protection of digital systems concerns a wide range of public services and organisations. In Germany, this cross-cutting nature of cybersecurity meets an already strongly subdivided structure of responsibilities in the area of security. Also, cybersecurity requires far greater cooperation between the state and business than traditional security policy challenges, since the majority of systems affected by cyber attacks are not within the state's sphere of responsibility. As a result, there are various forms of public-private cooperation. These factors lead to a confusing and immature allocation of cybersecurity responsibilities.

Keywords Federal Office for Information Security (BSI) · Law enforcement Intelligence service · Cyber command · Cyber Defence Centre · Public-private partnerships

4.1 Particularities of German Law Enforcement, Intelligence, and Public Security Organisations

In Germany's state organisation, responsibility for public security is spread across numerous different actors (Graulich 2016; Schönbohm et al. 2011, p. 71). Institutional separation rules characterise the landscape of internal security as well as sophisticated forms of cooperation rules. Two significant separations mark Germany's security architecture: the federal split between the federal and state governments and the functional split between police forces and intelligence services. The responsibility for police primarily lies with the Länder (states) with their 16 police organisations. The federal police organisations are relatively small and have limited powers. The focus of the intelligence services' work is on the federal level with domestic, foreign, and military intelligence services. By comparison, Länder's domestic intelligence services are relatively modest in terms of responsibilities and resources. While intelligence services are subject to mainly executive and, in the second-place, parliamentary con-

© The Author(s) 2018
M. Schallbruch and I. Skierka, *Cybersecurity in Germany*, SpringerBriefs
in Cybersecurity, https://doi.org/10.1007/978-3-319-90014-8_4

trol and oversight, police authorities' prosecution activities are supervised by the judiciary. This interferes with ministerial control of the police's hazard prevention activities. Some special regulatory agencies have police-like powers for certain areas of operation. Concerning cybersecurity, the Federal Office for Information Security (Bundesamt für Sicherheit in der Informationstechnik, BSI) should be mentioned first and foremost. However, the various supervisory agencies for critical infrastructures also have security tasks that now reach into cyberspace.

At the political level, the primary responsibility for internal security lies with the interior or home affairs ministers of the federal and Länder governments. They are in principle responsible for police forces and intelligence services; the ministries of justice have traditionally played a lesser operational role, despite their attorneys' duties as public prosecutors, but have an important role in the further development of internal security legislation due to their responsibilities in criminal law and criminal prosecution law. The Conference of Interior Ministers of the Länder (Innenminis-terkonferenz, IMK) plays an important role in coordinating national security policy. The Federal Minister of the Interior (Bundesminister des Innern, BMI) also attends the meetings. The conference and its various working groups decisively coordinate Germany's practical security policy (Hegele and Behnke 2017).

The BSI plays a unique role. It was established in 1991 by federal law (Gesetz über die Errichtung des Bundesamtes für Sicherheit in der Informationstechnik vom 17. Dezember 1990). It has the overall task of promoting the security of information technology (IT). As a result of several amendments to the law in 2009, 2015, and 2017, lawmakers successively extended the range of tasks, so that the BSI today assumes the function of a central cybersecurity authority in Germany. The BSI has neither police nor intelligence powers, but with regard to cyberspace, it fulfils both police and intelligence functions. The Office's mission can be divided into three areas in a very simplified way: Establishing and reviewing product and systems security, overseeing the implementation of cybersecurity measures, and operational cyber defence.

In the area of defining and testing product and system security, the BSI is initially the central accreditation and certification body for IT security in Germany. IT security certificates are only issued by BSI-accredited bodies. The BSI is also authorized to investigate the IT security of the market's products and services and may issue public warnings if a lack of IT security of products or services is detected. Wherever there is a statutory requirement for IT security in Germany, the legal provisions refer to the relevant guidelines or specifications of the BSI. Between 2013 and 2017 alone, 45 additional laws and regulations were adopted which entrusted the BSI with such tasks (Schallbruch 2017, p. 649). Thus, the BSI has acquired a kind of "official authority" in Germany over what secure information technology is and what not. The Office's second area of responsibility concerns the supervision of the implementation of cybersecurity measures. Historically, the BSI has always carried out this task for crypto devices that protect state secrets. They have been approved by the BSI since the Office was established. This competency was successively extended, most recently by the IT security law to the entire area of critical infrastructures. The mostly private operators of the infrastructures have to protect their relevant IT systems against cyber attacks according to the "state of the art" and have to prove this to the BSI. If the security measures are not sufficient, BSI can issue complaints and impose fines. In parallel to competencies concerning critical infrastructure security, Germany has also delegated enforcement powers for digital services (online marketplaces, search engines, and cloud services) regulated by the European Network and Information Security (NIS) Directive to the BSI (Schallbruch 2017b , p. 800). As a result, the Office can take up cybersecurity issues for almost any relevant form of technology through its investigation and warning competencies and address them by means of penalties or public notices. Thus, the BSI has an extremely high level of duty to keep an eye on the entire realm of IT security, especially since the BSI is legally obliged, at least vis-à-vis the critical infrastructures, to issue a warning without delay if relevant security evidence is available (Sect. 8a.2 No. 4 BSI Act). If the BSI neglects this obligation, liability claims against the state are conceivable.

The third area of responsibility of the BSI is cyber defence. Since 2009, the Office has been responsible for supporting the federal government authorities in fending off cyber attacks. To this end, the BSI monitors the federal government's networks, investigates security incidents and takes defensive measures. However, active operations outside the federal networks are in general not permitted for the BSI. Here, the Office must cooperate with the public prosecutors' offices and police forces. Since 2015, the BSI has also been involved in the cyber defence of critical infrastructure operators. They must report cybersecurity incidents to the agency, which draws up a situation report from them and in turn helps companies to defend themselves by providing them with information. The German implementation law of the EU NIS Directive has extended this task: Due to the newly created Section 5a of the BSI Act, the Office is now also entitled to help with cyber defence at the request of a critical infrastructure operator. However, this new power is limited to the systems concerned. The BSI does not have any further (police) powers outside of these systems, i.e. within provider or telecom networks. Here the BSI has to ask the competent police department for help. All in all, however, the BSI has meanwhile assumed a central position for cybersecurity in Germany due to the multitude of new responsibilities that government and parliament assigned to the agency (Bötticher 2015, p. 90).

The police powers in Germany are exercised primarily by the Länder with the sixteen state police forces. They form the backbone of the German police force. The federal police authorities, the Federal Police (Bundespolizei), the Federal Criminal Police Office (Bundeskriminalamt, BKA) and the Customs Investigation Bureau (Zollkriminalamt, ZKA) are only responsible for specific issues. As a rule, prosecution for cyber attacks is a matter for the state police under the supervision of the local public prosecutor's office. Many Länder have set up so-called focal public prosecutors' offices for cyber crime, e.g. the state of Lower Saxony (Innenministerium Niedersachsen 2011). Most Länder have also set up central units for cyber crime at their state criminal police offices, which are typically tasked by public prosecutors with cyber-related investigations. At the federal level, the Federal Criminal Police Office (BKA) is particularly important. The Federal Police is primarily a protective police force with responsibilities for border security, airports, and railway police and has only marginal duties in the area of cybersecurity. The Customs Investigation Bureau (ZKA), as the financial police in particular, also plays no significant role in cybersecurity.

The BKA has the role of a core unit of the German police, which collects and processes information on a national basis. Accordingly, the BKA publishes annual federal situation reports on cyber crime (Bundeskriminalamt 2016). However, the Office also has its own cybersecurity powers. According to Sect. 4.1 No. 5 of the BKA Act, the Office is also responsible for cyber crime if attackers target the federal government or critical infrastructures. In this case, the appropriate prosecutor's office in the respective Land entrusts the BKA with the investigation. However, the investigation capabilities of the BKA in cyberspace are very limited. New investigative powers such as source telecommunications monitoring and secret access to IT systems (i.e. online searches), which the BKA received in 2017, may only be used for particular crimes. Cyber attacks are only part of this if they are in the context of espionage. The BKA has no authority in the field of cybersecurity to prevent threats, i.e. to act in the run-up to a criminal offence. It's the state police that is in charge here.

With the Federal Office for the Protection of the Constitution (Bundesamt für Verfassungsschutz, BfV) and the constitutional protection offices of the federal states, Germany has 17 domestic intelligence services. Besides, there is the Military Counter-Intelligence Service (Militärischer Abschirmdienst, MAD), which is, however, only responsible for activities against the German Armed Forces or those involving Bundeswehr personnel. The Federal Office for the Protection of the Constitution is mainly concerned with the investigation of right-wing and left-wing extremism, foreigners' extremism, and terrorism. However, their responsibility for counterintelligence also plays an important role in the area of cybersecurity. According to the Federal Office's observations, foreign intelligence services increasingly carry out their espionage activities digitally. According to the BfV, Germany is the target of numerous cyber espionage attacks of Russian and Chinese origin in particular, but frequently also from Iran (Bundesministerium des Innern and "Verfassungsschutzbericht 2016, p. 260). In the context of cybersecurity, it is also the task of the Federal Office for the Protection (BfV) of the Constitution to collect information about attacks and attackers from open sources as well as by means of intelligence resources. The Office for the Protection of the Constitution is entitled to support cyber defence. However, it has no police powers and may not carry out searches or arrests. This restriction is the result of strict segregation of police and intelligence powers. Following the experience with the secret state police of the Nazi dictatorship, the Allied forces introduced a so-called separation order as a condition for drafting the (West) German constitution after World War II. The order of 1949 has constitutional status and also limits the personal, organisational and informational cooperation between the police and the intelligence services (Fremuth 2014).

The division of responsibilities between the federal and state constitutional protection authorities is not entirely clear. Both the BfV and the state authorities are responsible for counterintelligence. The federal office is not only responsible for coordinating the Länder offices, but also has independent powers in the case of efforts directed against the federal republic, extending beyond the area of a Land or concerning Germany's foreign affairs (Sect. 5.1 of the Federal Constitution Protection Act). All of these prerequisites may be present in a cyber attack. In the event of a cyber attack against a federal agency, such as the attack against the federal government's network in the winter of 2018, the competence of the federal office is obvious. The situation is different in the case of attacks against businesses, for example. When a cyber attack is detected, neither the originator nor the objective of the attack can typically be identified. Responsibilities of state and federal domestic intelligence services are widely parallel. Accordingly, the federal and state offices must consult each other on a case-by-case basis. The federal office has no right to steer the state offices. The BfV has a specialized group for electronic attacks. Some Länder have also set up specialised organisational units in their constitutional protection agencies, such as Bavaria. With its Cyber-Alliance Centre established specifically for this purpose, the Bavarian State Office for the Protection of the Constitution is in charge of defending even against cyber attacks on the private sector (Bayerisches Staatsministerium des Innern et al. 2013). Other Länder have refrained from doing so. Some states such as North Rhine-Westphalia and Bavaria have also given an authorization to secretly intrude into IT systems to the intelligence services [e.g. Section 5.2 No. 11 VSG NW (Gesetz über den Verfassungsschutz in Nordrhein-Westfalen (Verfassungsschutzgesetz Nordrhein- Westfalen - VSG NW -) vom 20.12 1994) or Article 10 BayVSG (Bayerisches Verfassungsschutzgesetz (BayVSG) 2016)]. The BfV has no such right. At federal level, only the BKA is entitled to do so.

With the Federal Intelligence Service (Bundesnachrichtendienst, BND), Germany has a single foreign intelligence service, which also performs the function of a military intelligence service abroad. The Federal Chancellery steers its operations. The BND's mission is to collect a wide range of security-relevant information abroad. For this purpose, it uses standard intelligence tools, human sources (HUMINT), open sources of information (OSINT) as well as signals intelligence generated by the monitoring of electronic communications (SIGINT). The Federal Chancellery defines the specific objectives of the BND in a so-called "mission profile". The Bundestag redefined the BND's powers in 2016, not least concerning electronic cooperation with foreign intelligence services such as the US National Security Agency (Karl/Soigne 2017). In the future, the BND will also increasingly focus on supporting cyber defence within the scope of its powers to monitor electronic communications. As part of the task called "SIGINT Support to Cyber Defence (SSCD)", the BND collects information abroad on current or upcoming cyber attacks, malware, etc. (Bundesnachrichtendienst 2018). Active cyber defence activities such as Cyber Networks Operations (CNO) are not a task of the BND.

In the context of cybersecurity in critical infrastructures, the supervisory agencies established for each sector also have a role to play. Some infrastructure sectors are in principle subject to federal supervision, such as energy supply, telecommunications or finance, while the Länder authorities largely supervise other sectors such as health care, food supply, or transport. All sectoral supervisory authorities are usually also responsible for the proper functioning of the infrastructure sectors. With respect to cybersecurity issues, they operate alongside the BSI. The role of the supervisory authorities is more significant if they have their own sectoral statutory powers for cyber, such as in the energy supply, telecommunications, or finance sectors. The agencies operating there, such as the Bundesnetzagentur (BNetzA) for telecommunications and energy or the Federal Financial Supervisory Authority (Bundesanstalt für Finanzdienstleistungsaufsicht, BAFin), receive reports of cyber attacks in parallel with the BSI and may impose severe sanctions against companies that do not comply with their security obligations. In addition to the sectoral supervisory authorities, the Federal Government runs a Federal Office of Civil Protection and Disaster Assistance (Bundesamt für Bevölkerungsschutz und Katastrophenhilfe, BBK), which plays a coordinating role in the area of critical infrastructures and also conducts regular crisis exercises, including those in the field of cyber defence. As early as 2011, the federal and state authorities had already trained in an exercise called "LÜKEX 2011" to deal with a cyber attack. Approximately 3000 persons in various agencies, the German Armed Forces, and 45 critical infrastructure companies were involved in a table-top exercise under the direction of the National Crisis Management Group in the BMI (Bundesamt für Bevölkerungsschutz und Katastrophenhilfe and "Auswertungsbericht LÜKEX 2011). In 2020, another large-scale Bund-Länder cyber exercise is to take place, this time with the scenario of a cyber attack on critical infrastructures and the problem of maintaining government functions (Innenministerkonferenz 2017, p. 24).

4.2 The German Military's Role in the Cyber Realm

The German Bundeswehr is a defence army and a parliamentary army. Its fields of operation are very limited by the German constitution. Also, deployments require the explicit approval of the German Bundestag. The main purpose of the Bundeswehr is to defend Germany against armed attacks from outside. Beyond defence, the military may only be deployed in narrowly defined cases, which are expressly regulated by the constitution ("Verfassungsrechtliche Regeln für Cyberoperationen der Bundeswehr 2017). The German constitution makes a differentiation between the Bundeswehr's intervention below the threshold of deployment and explicit deployments approved by parliament. Below the threshold, the German Armed Forces can, for example, take measures to secure themselves in the cyber sector. They are, however, limited because they do not allow any interference with the legal rights of third parties, i.e. no access to computer systems outside the German armed forces' networks. Cases of cyber defence, in which the German Armed Forces provide assistance to other authorities within the framework of their powers (so-called administrative assistance), are not regarded as deployments. The Bundeswehr could, for example, support the BSI or the police forces in cyber defence activities on a selective and individual basis. However, administrative assistance is not sufficient as a legal basis for lasting institutionalised cooperation in which the military itself takes over cyber defence measures (Marxsen 2017, p. 546).

Cyber defence operations carried out under its own responsibility and affecting third parties must, in any case, be characterised as a deployment of the German Federal Armed Forces. It needs a legal basis for this. For domestic missions, only the competence of the German Armed Forces for defence is applicable. A prerequisite for this is an armed attack on the federal territory. It must be essentially the same as a military attack, both regarding its effects and its originator, a foreign state. Other cyber attacks fall within the competence of internal security authorities (Marxsen 2017, p. 548). Besides, the Bundeswehr would always need parliamentary approval for cyber defence missions. No problem at all is the execution of cyber operations within the framework of foreign missions of the German Federal Armed Forces, for which a mandate of the UN, NATO, or EU exists and which the Bundestag has approved. In this context, not only conventional weapons may be used, but cyber operations may be carried out as well.

The legal framework for the deployment of the German Federal Armed Forces in cyber defence is thus considerably restricted. The Bundeswehr will only be able to fend off cyber attacks in Germany if it can record a clearly belligerent cyber operation and obtain the approval of the Bundestag. Accordingly, the Bundeswehr has set up only tiny forces for Cyber Network Operations (CNO). They have never been deployed a single time, at least until 2015 (Bundesministerium der Verteidigung et al. 2015, p. 3). At the same time, however, the cyber domain has developed internationally as a central field of action for the military, without the threshold of armed attacks being typically surpassed. The Bundeswehr, too, must prepare itself for this because it has to carry out cyber operations within the framework of mandates, at least for its own security and also for the preparation of missions abroad. Therefore, the development of cyber skills is an explicit will of the German government (Bundesministerium des Innern 2016a, p. 33).

Based on this demand, in 2017 the German Armed Forces set up a "Command Cyber and Information Space" (Kommando Cyber- und Informationsraum, CIR), a separate military operational area for operations in cyberspace. Some 14,000 soldiers are expected to be deployed. A large part of the posts are transferred from existing units. Only 300 additional posts are planned (Bundesministerium der Verteidigung et al. 2016, p. 22). The concept of the CIR command follows a comprehensive approach to combine all forces needed for the reconnaissance, operation, and management of cyberspace in one military organisational area. The mission includes the handling of communications as well as the operation of command support systems, the protection of the Bundeswehr's IT systems against attacks as well as the execution of cyber network operations within the framework of deployments. In the new structure, the Centre for Communications and the Centre for Geoinformation Systems for the Information supply, the Bundeswehr IT Centre (IT-Zentrum Bw) for systems operation, the Centre for Cybersecurity of the Bundeswehr (Zentrum für Cybersicherheit der Bundeswehr, ZCSBw) for the protection of its own systems and the Centre for Cyber Operation (Zentrum für Cyber-Operationen, ZCO) for CNO are responsible (Bundesministerium der Verteidigung et al. 2016). The expansion of training and research activities at the Bundeswehr University in Munich supports the further development of the Bundeswehr's cyber capabilities (Bundesministerium der Verteidigung et al. 2016, pp. 33–35).

With the CIR command, the Bundeswehr has taken a significant organisational step towards strengthening military cybersecurity in Germany. The efficacy cannot yet be estimated. The consequences of the organisational restructuring will not be noticeable until a few years from now. Moreover, the cyber forces have not yet been significantly strengthened (Zedler 2017, p. 74).

4.3 Cooperation and Conflict Between Agencies

Cybersecurity is not easy to locate in the complex distribution of responsibilities among authorities with security tasks in Germany. Both the federal and state civil security authorities and the military have tasks and powers in cyberspace. They range from intelligence and investigation measures in the run-up to cyber threats (intelligence services, BSI, Bundeswehr) to the definition and control of protective measures (BSI, supervisory agencies) and the protection of own infrastructures (BSI, Bundeswehr), the concrete prevention of hazards in the event of cyber attacks (police, BSI) up to prosecution (police) and finally the defence of Germany against warlike cyber attacks (Bundeswehr). In many cases, it is difficult to determine which authority is responsible in an individual case, because different bodies can claim responsibility under certain perspectives.

This claim is particularly evident in the case of cyber defence, for example in the case of severe attacks against state institutions such as the federal government's computer network at the beginning of 2018 (Deutsche Welle 2018). BSI is responsible for protecting the federal government's IT, including government networks. Due to the apparent allegations of espionage, the BfV is also responsible. Because the attackers targeted a federal institution, the BKA is responsible for criminal prosecution (on behalf of the attorney general). Finally, with regard to the power of protection of its own networks and capabilities, the Bundeswehr, which is at least marginally affected by the attack, also has responsibilities in this case - it also uses the attacked computer network for its own purposes. In the specific case, Länder authorities are not involved. This would be different if not the federal government but, for example, a critical infrastructure were attacked.

An explicit allocation of competence to only one authority is not possible in the system of German security authorities. This is due to the nature of cyber attacks. When a cyber attack is discovered, typically neither the originator of the attack nor its target can be identified. Also, in the first few days after the discovery of a possible attack, the focus is still on the containment of the attack, the analysis of the scope of the affected systems, and, if necessary, the restarting of the systems. These tasks, which are—especially if they are to be carried out in the networks of private companies—not of classical police or intelligence nature, they are most suitable for the technical focus of the BSI.

In June 2011 the federal government established a National Cyber Defence Centre (Cyber-Abwehrzentrum, Cyber-AZ). The Centre is an attempt to coordinate the multiple responsibilities of the authorities and create a joint information and exchange platform. The Cyber-AZ is part of the BSI. It is staffed by civil servants from the BSI, the BfV, and the BBK. Liaison officers ensure the exchange with the BKA and the Federal Police. In some cases, the BND, the ZKA, and the various facilities of the Bundeswehr also cooperate (Bötticher 2015, p. 91; Graulich 2016, p. 776). Supervisory authorities from the federal government are also successively integrated, for example, the Federal Financial Supervisory Authority BAFin (Bundesanstalt für Finanzdienstleistungsaufsicht 2018). The Cyber Defence Centre has no independent competences and powers. All powers remain with the authorities involved. Cyber-AZ only coordinates their cooperation. The Cyber-AZ was inspired by the Joint Terrorism Defence Centre (Gemeinsames Terrorismus-Abwehrzentrum, GTAZ), in which federal and state authorities from the police and the Office for the Protection of the Constitution have been working together since 2008. However, the GTAZ has a staff of 200 employees, while only 10 permanent employees work in the Cyber-AZ (Linke 2015, p. 130). The effectiveness of the Cyber Defence Centre is not only being called into question in the public eye. The Federal Audit Office (Bundesrechnungshof, BRH) also criticised the establishment and lack of effectiveness of the centre in 2014: It would not be in a position to pool the fragmented competencies and capabilities for cyber defence (Goetz and Leyendecker 2014). Three years later, this finding has been confirmed by representatives of the security agencies (Zedler 2017, p. 75), even though many cyber defence operations have been coordinated there in the meantime (Bundesamt für Sicherheit in der Informationstechnik, "Pressemitteilung 'BSI ermöglicht Zerschlagung der Botnetz-Infrastruktur Avalanche'," 01 December 2016). However, the government has neither given significantly more personnel to the defence centre nor independent responsibilities and powers. Due to the constitutional situation, the latter would only be possible in Germany through a law. However, with legal regulation of the Cyber-AZ, the information cooperation between intelligence services and the police in the centre would have to be formally described in detail – concerning the separation requirement (Linke 2015). Therefore, to avoid bureaucratic procedures, politics has so far refrained from doing so. The Cyber-AZ also has limited capacity for coordination and information exchange. Neither the private sector is represented in the Cyber-AZ, nor even the critical infrastructures. Neither are the Länder involved nor are they linked in any way. The federal government must implement the Länder participation in the future, in line with the NCSS 2016 (Bundesministerium des Innern 2016a, p. 27).

The assignment of tasks and cooperation between the federal government and the Länder in cybersecurity as a whole has not yet been clearly defined. It is true that the representatives of the Länder join the National Cybersecurity Council, which has been responsible for strategic cybersecurity issues since the 2011 national cybersecurity strategy under the leadership of the BMI. However, it has not yet achieved any notable overall effectiveness, not even in federal-state coordination. The powerful conference of interior ministers (Innenministerkonferenz) continues to dominate here (Hegele and Behnke 2017), which periodically deals with cybersecurity issues and has set up a working group for this purpose (Innenministerkonferenz 2017, p. 5). However, the organisational structure, which also differs widely from state to state, makes coordination considerably more difficult than in the case of police forces and intelligence services. Bavaria, for example, is the first German state to establish its own State Office for Information Security (Landesamt für Sicherheit in der Informationstechnik, LSI). On the one hand, it is responsible for primary Bavarian tasks such as the protection of the state's IT systems; on the other hand, it also has duties that overlap with the activities of the BSI, such as advising industry and critical infrastructures (Landesamt für Sicherheit in der Informationstechnik 2018). Other Länder refrain from having own authorities and instead enter into cooperation agreements with the BSI. In addition, cooperation between the federal government and the Länder is made more difficult by the fact that, in addition to coordination within the Cybersecurity Council and the Conference of Interior Ministers with the IT Planning Council (IT-Planungsrat), there is a third federal and state body responsible for cybersecurity issues. Its responsibility is the cooperation between the federal government and the Länder in the security of the state's IT systems (Schallbruch 2017, p. 654).

Civil-military cooperation on cybersecurity has been optimised, at least from the military side, by setting up the CIR command. A unified organisation and the concentration of supervision of all cybersecurity issues in the Cyber and Information Technology directorate general of the Federal Ministry of Defence make military cyber defence more willing to cooperate with the civilian side (Bundesministerium der Verteidigung et al. 2016, p. 18). At the same time, the Ministry of Defence has always emphasised in the reorganisation process that the leadership of the Ministry of the Interior for cybersecurity should remain in place. The Bundeswehr has created the conditions for intensive civil-military cooperation in the past few years. However, shortcomings in the cybersecurity cooperation between government agencies in Germany continue to exist between the various civil authorities of the federal government and in unsettled federal-state collaboration.

4.4 Public-Private Cybersecurity Cooperation

In general, cyberspace is privately owned. Major digital infrastructures such as backbone networks or critical infrastructure IT systems belong to private companies. Innovations in the cyberspace are the result of the market-driven development of private-sector products and business models. The global interconnection of the digitalized world is not driven by state actors, but by the private sector. Like almost all national cybersecurity strategies (Carr 2016, p. 44) the German cybersecurity strategy also emphasises the need for "trusting cooperation and close exchange" between the state and industry as a prerequisite for sustainable cybersecurity (Bundesministerium des Innern 2016a, p. 21). Since 2005, various forms of cooperation between the state and industry have developed in Germany for this purpose, which more or less successfully see cybersecurity as a joint task. In some cases they are highly institutionalized, in others, they consist only of loose agreements between public and private actors.

The different approaches to public-private cooperation can be broadly broken down into four different areas, depending on the degree of commitment: (1) the joint organisation of responsibility for cybersecurity in a sector, (2) platforms and formats for exchanging operational cybersecurity information, (3) cooperation formats for preventive cybersecurity, and (4) forms of cooperation for the dissemination of cybersecurity know-how to the public.

In the *first area of cooperation*, the organisation of joint responsibility between the state and the private sector, the so-called UP KRITIS is the oldest and most important partnership. It was founded in 2007 on the initiative of the federal government together with critical infrastructure operators in order to secure the cybersecurity of critical infrastructures. UP KRITIS stands for "Implementation Plan Critical Infrastructures" (Bundesministerium des Innern 2007) and is an outcome of the first German cybersecurity strategy 2005, which had adopted a cooperative approach to the protection of cybersecurity critical infrastructures and provided for the necessary measures to be defined by an agreement between government and industry (Bundesministerium des Innern 2005, p. 8). The UP KRITIS serves this purpose, but it was more than just a declaration. Besides, there was an exchange and coordination platform with initially 40 participants. These included individual infrastructure operators such as Deutsche Bahn as well as industry associations such as the German Insurance Association. BSI, BBK, and also the Bundesbank represented the public side in the UP KRITIS. BMI acted as a chair of the platform. In the meantime, the BSI has taken over the coordination and administration of the growing platform. At the beginning of 2018, it counted 540 participants (UP KRITIS-Geschäftsstelle 2017). Initially, the motives of the government and the private sector to participate in UP KRITIS were very similar: reducing complexity. Having a lack of knowledge about the IT security of critical infrastructures, the government had a need for reliable assessments and for a certain degree of expressiveness towards the public. Given the diversity of supervisory and security authorities in the federal and state governments, companies wanted to ensure that their relations with the state would be able to meet a certain degree of reliability, which protected their business from surprises (Freiberg 2016, p. 112).

The UP KRITIS has developed a wide variety of activities according to the mutual interest in making the other side more transparent. From the beginning, four working groups dealt with identifying cross-sector critical dependencies between infrastructures, defining crisis management processes in the event of cyber attacks, preparing joint exercises and exchanging views on EU activities and EU legislation. The UP KRITIS has produced many practical results, such as the establishment of sectoral Single Points of Contact for the exchange of situational information or the joint implementation of the exercise LÜKEX 2011. However, it was not possible to broaden the cooperation in such a way that all critical infrastructure sectors became involved in the partnership. As a result of a detailed analysis of IT security of critical infrastructures conducted in 2012, the BMI found that the voluntary approach "did not have a nationwide impact in all security-related areas" (Bundesamt für Sicherheit in der Informationstechnik 2017, p. 9) and presented the draft of a law. Though the government turned down the purely voluntary cooperation, the mutual trust that had developed as a result of the close collaboration in UP KRITIS also survived this strategic change. The government also made efforts to support this and incorporated key findings of the UP KRITIS into the legal regulations and the implementation of the law. An example is the provision in Sect. 8a.2 of the IT Security Act, according to which BSI can recognize industry standards that are drawn up by critical infrastructure operators as a fulfilment of legal obligations. Usually, the industry working groups of UP KRITIS are developing such standards (UP KRITIS-Geschäftsstelle 2017). In addition, the working groups of UP KRITIS were closely involved in the development of the legal provisions with which the Federal Government determined which operators fall under the IT security law (Referentenentwurf des BMI - Entwurf einer Verordnung zur Bestimmung kritischer Infrastrukturen nach dem BSI-Gesetz 2016, p. 1).

Following this, UP KRITIS developed from a voluntary public-private partnership to a cooperation platform of state and critical infrastructures, which operates within the framework of legal regulations and supports its implementation. It also provides additional cooperation contributions that are not regulated by the legislator, such as the organisation of crisis management processes and the preparation of exercises. In 14 industry working groups and nine thematic working groups, the state and industry are engaged in improving the cybersecurity of critical infrastructures (Bundesamt für Sicherheit in der Informationstechnik 2017, p. 19). The cooperation is widely viewed as being beneficial by both sides (Zedler 2017, p. 77; Bundesamt für Sicherheit in der Informationstechnik 2017, p. 21).

Less institutionalized cooperation exists between the government and the internet providers in Germany. The collaboration between security agencies and providers is particularly important in the defence against ongoing cyber attacks. For instance, the government regularly provides internet providers with information about systems and users affected by cyber attacks on their networks, e.g. in the event of a case of millions of identities stolen in 2014 (Bundesamt für Sicherheit in der Informationstechnik 2014) or the takedown of the Avalanche botnet in 2016 (Bundesamt für Sicherheit in der Informationstechnik 2016). The close cooperation has led to the federal government's adoption of special powers for providers to defend against cyber threats in the new law on the implementation of the EU NIS Directive adopted in 2017. Section 109a of the Telecommunications Act has since permitted the blocking of users who are part of a botnet or the redirection of data traffic to so-called sinkhole servers. The state and telecoms are thus taking joint responsibility for the security of internet infrastructures.

The *second field of cooperation* between government and business is the exchange of operational information on cyber defence. The IT Security Act introduced very formal reporting obligations for infrastructure operators that are affected by cyber attacks. Also, various more informal exchange platforms have developed in Germany. One of these is the German Competence Centre against Cyber Crime (G4C) (German Competence Centre against Cyber Crime," [Online]. Available: http://www.g4c-ev.or g/. Accessed 06 03 2018). The BKA together with companies from the financial sector founded the association. It is inspired by the American National Cyber Forensics & Training Alliance (NCFTA). In the meantime, BSI is also involved. At a joint location in Wiesbaden, government officials and corporate employees work together to analyse and solve cyber attacks, especially in the field of phishing.

The German Cybersecurity Organisation (Deutsche Cyber-Sicherheits-organisation, DCSO) is pursuing an even more far-reaching cooperation approach. It was founded in the form of a private, non-profit-making company by a group of large DAX companies. Core areas are the exchange of information on vulnerabilities, exploits, attack vectors and specific attacks, the assessment of attacks as well as the joint security assessment of IT products and services. DCSO exchanges information with the BSI. BMI and BSI are represented in the company's boards (Deutsche Cyber-Sicherheitsorganisation 2016). For the operational exchange of cybersecurity information, there are also a number of other agreements, mainly bilateral contracts and platforms between public authorities and private companies. With the 2016 national cybersecurity strategy (NCSS), the federal government announces the creation of a unified cooperation platform for this purpose (Bundesministerium des Innern 2016a, p. 25).

The *third area of cooperation* between government and industry in the field of cybersecurity is dedicated above all to the development of preventive assistance, exchange, and advice. Here, several different forms of cooperation have arisen which have similar objectives, overlapping groups of participants but slightly different priorities. The reasons for this diversity are the mostly parallel initiatives of various government agencies to establish exchange platforms for cybersecurity together with industry. At the action of the BSI, the Alliance for Cybersecurity was established in 2012. BMI and BSI together with some trade associations jointly support it. By 2018 the association already has 2600 members, mainly individual companies, but also a large number of public authorities. Within the alliance, the members exchange non-operational cybersecurity information. The services include, for example, a monthly IT security status report provided by the BSI. Alliance participants can also submit their own materials, such as guidelines and information sheets. Expert circles and advanced training seminars complete the offer (Federal Office for Information Security 2014).

At the initiative of the Federal Ministry of Economics and Energy (Bundesministerium für Wirtschaft und Energie, BMWi), the Task Force "IT Security in Business" was set up—at the same time as the NCSS 2011. Meanwhile renamed "Initiative IT security in Business", the primary goal of the cooperation between BMWi and business enterprises is to increase IT security in small and medium-sized enterprises. The initiative does not have a membership structure like the Alliance for Cybersecurity. It is more a funding programme that the ministry, together with experts and representatives from industry, has conceived and implemented. Results include, for example, technical tools for SMEs to check their websites, specific seminars, targeted awareness-raising activities for particular groups such as the craft trades and freelance professions, or the involvement of multipliers in cybersecurity such as tax advisors or auditors (Bundesministerium für Wirtschaft und Energie, "Initiative IT-Sicherheit in der Wirtschaft," [Online]. Available: http://www.it-sicherheit-in-der-wirtschaft.de/IT-Sicherheit/Navigation/root.html. Accessed 06 03 2018). In contrast to the Alliance for Cybersecurity, which aims at an open and comprehensive exchange of experience and information between government and business, the initiative focuses very strongly on SMEs.

Finally, it is worth mentioning the "Initiative for Business Protection" (Initiative Wirtschaftsschutz), which was founded mainly on the initiative of the BfV. Supporter of this interchange platform are the federal security agencies BfV, BKA, BND, and BSI as well as the umbrella organisations of the German business community (BDI and DIHK) and other business associations. It aims to intensify cooperation between government and industry to protect German companies against industrial espionage, sabotage and other forms of crime (Zedler 2017, p. 76). The platform is a part of a national business protection strategy jointly presented by government and industry (Bundesministerium des Innern 2016). However, the strategy itself has never been published. Although the BSI is cooperating, information on cybersecurity is hard to find on the platform of the "Initiative Wirtschaftsschutz", apparently to differentiate it from the Alliance for Cybersecurity. The effectiveness of this public-private partnership (PPP) for cybersecurity is currently difficult to assess.

Finally, the *fourth area of cooperation* between government and industry in Germany in the field of cybersecurity is to be noted: joint information, advice, and support for citizens concerning cyberspace threats. A not-for-profit association founded in 2006, "Deutschland sicher im Netz e. V." (DsiN) is under the patronage of the BMI. Its members are some bigger companies, mainly from the ICT industry, and a few NGOs. DsiN provides a wide range of information about security on the Internet and carries out projects to bring certain target groups to IT security, such as pupils, seniors, parents or users of certain Internet services. (Deutschland sicher im Netz e.V. 2016). There are several similar initiatives such as "Deutschland sicher im Netz", both nationwide and at the state level.

In no other field of security policy has the German state entered into so many partnerships with the private sector. In total, many thousands of public and private institutions are in some way involved in PPPs on cybersecurity. Almost every aspect of the implementation of the government's cybersecurity strategy is accompanied or supported by cooperation with industry. In the light of the linkage between public and private responsibility, there is probably no alternative. With the various PPPs, especially at federal level, however, the state also transfers its deficits in cooperation and coordination of cybersecurity to the private sector. Many of the initiatives work largely in parallel, often with similar actors. The German Armed Forces, which found its position in cyberspace very late in the game, is also seeking to be close to the world of business, for example by setting up a Cyber Innovation Hub to connect military demand with business innovation.

While cooperation in the protection of critical infrastructures seems to be organized adequately by the UP KRITIS, there is still no robust exchange of operational cyber defence information between the state and industry. Neither the Alliance for Cybersecurity nor smaller entities such as G4C and DCSO adequately cover the interest of companies in quickly obtaining high-quality information from security agencies on vulnerabilities, attack vectors and cyber situation to protect themselves. There is a definite need for improvement here, especially since the amount of information accumulated by the government is steadily increasing: at BSI from mandatory reporting requirements and legally stipulated product tests, at the intelligence services from the expanded powers to investigate cyberspace.

Germany has worked very intensively on building public-private partnerships for cybersecurity but has not yet found a sustainable long-term solution.

References

Bundesministerium des Innern (2007) Umsetzungsplan KRITIS des Nationalen Plans zum Schutz der Informationsinfrastrukturen, Berlin
Bundesministerium des Innern (2005) Nationaler Plan zum Schutz der Informationsinfrastrukturen (NPSI), Berlin
Bayerisches Staatsministerium des Innern, "Regierungserklärung des Bayerischen Staatsministers des Innern, Joachim Herrmann," 11 April 2013. [Online]. Available: https://www.stmi.bayern. de/assets/stmi/med/reden/stm_reg-erklaerung_cybersicherheit_130411.pdf. Accessed 05 March 2018
Bayerisches Verfassungsschutzgesetz (BayVSG) vom 12. Juli (2016) GVBl. Bayern, p S. 145
Bötticher A (2015) Strukturlandschaft der Inneren Sicherheit, in Cybersicherheit, Wiesbaden, Springer VS, pp 69–102
Bundesamt für Sicherheit in der Informationstechnik, "Pressemitteilung 'Neuer Fall von großflächigem Identitätsdiebstahl: BSI informiert Betroffene'," 07 April 2014. [Online]. Available: https://www.bsi.bund.de/DE/Presse/Pressemitteilungen/Presse2014/Neuer_Fall_von_Iden titaetsdiebstahl_07042014.html. Accessed 06 March 2018
Bundesamt für Sicherheit in der Informationstechnik, "Pressemitteilung 'BSI ermöglicht Zerschlagung der Botnetz-Infrastruktur Avalanche'," 01 December 2016. [Online]. Available: https://www.bsi.bund.de/DE/Presse/Pressemitteilungen/Presse2016/Botnetz_Avalanche_0 1122016.html. Accessed 06 March 2018

Bundesanstalt für Finanzdienstleistungsaufsicht, "Presseerklärung 'BaFin arbeitet im Nationalen Cyber-Abwehrzentrum mit'," [Online]. Available: https://www.bafin.de/SharedDocs/Veroeff entlichungen/DE/Pressemitteilung/2017/pm_170331_cyber-abwehrzentrum.html. Accessed 05 March 2018

Bundesamt für Sicherheit in der Informationstechnik, "Schutz Kritischer Infrastrukturen durch IT-Sicherheitsgesetz und UP KRITIS," 2017. [Online]. Available: https://www.bsi.bund.de/Shar edDocs/Downloads/DE/BSI/Publikationen/Broschueren/Schutz-Kritischer-Infrastrukturen-ITSi g-u-UP-KRITIS.pdf. Accessed 06 March 2018

Bundeskriminalamt (2018) Bundeslagebild Cyber Crime [Online]. Available: https://www. bka.de/DE/AktuelleInformationen/StatistikenLagebilder/Lagebilder/Cyber   crime/cyber crime_node.html. Accessed 05 March 2018

Bundesministerium der Verteidigung (2015) Antwort auf die Kleine Anfrage "Elektronische Kampf-führung der Bundeswehr", Deutscher Bundestag, *Drucksache* 18/3963

Bundesministerium der Verteidigung (2016) Abschlussbericht Aufbaustab Cyber- und Informationsraum, Bonn

Bundesministerium des Innern (2016a) Cyber-Sicherheitsstrategie für Deutschland, Berlin

Bundesministerium des Innern (2016b) Referentenentwurf des BMI - Entwurf einer Verordnung zur Bestimmung kritischer Infrastrukturen nach dem BSI-Gesetz, 13 01 2016. [Online]. Available: https://www.bmi.bund.de/SharedDocs/downloads/DE/gesetztestexte/gesetzestentwuerfe/k ritis-vo-entwurf.html. Accessed 06 March 2018

Bundesministerium des Innern, "Bundessicherheitsbehörden und Verbände ziehen an einem Strang. Nationale Wirtschaftsschutzstrategie vorgestellt.," 26 04 2016. [Online]. Available: https://www.bmi.bund.de/SharedDocs/pressemitteilungen/DE/2016/04/nationale-wirtscha ftsschutzstrategie-vorgestellt.html. Accessed 06 March 2018

Bundesministerium für Wirtschaft und Energie, "Initiative IT-Sicherheit in der Wirtschaft," [Online]. Available: http://www.it-sicherheit-in-der-wirtschaft.de/IT-Sicherheit/Navigation/root. html. Accessed 06 March 2018

Bundesamt für Bevölkerungsschutz und Katastrophenhilfe, "Auswertungsbericht LÜKEX 2011. IT-Sicherheit in Deutschland.," 2012. [Online]. Available: https://www.bbk.bund.de/SharedDocs/Do wnloads/BBK/DE/Publikationen/Broschueren_Flyer/Luekex_11_Auswertung.pdf. Accessed 05 March 2018

Bundesministerium des Innern (2017) Verfassungsschutzbericht 2016, Berlin

Bundesnachrichtendienst (2018) "Cyber-Sicherheit – Sicherung der nationalen Informationstechnik in Zeiten globaler Vernetzung," [Online]. Available: http://www.bnd.bund.de/DE/Themen/Lage beitraege/Cyber-Sicherheit/Cyber-Sicherheit_node.html. Accessed 05 March 2018

Carr M (2016) Public-private partnerships in national cyber-security strategies. Int Aff 92(1):43–62

Deutsche Cyber-Sicherheitsorganisation, "Deutsche Cyber-Sicherheitsorganisation unterstützt Unternehmen bei Abwehr von Gefahren aus dem Netz," 19 August 2016. [Online]. Available: https://www.presseportal.de/pm/121523/3407438. Accessed 06 March 2018

Deutschland sicher im Netz e.V. (2016) "Jahresbericht 2016," 03 2017. [Online]. Available: https://www.sicher-im-netz.de/sites/default/files/download/dsin-jahresbericht_2016_web. pdf. Accessed 06 March 2018

Deutsche Welle (2018) "Germany admits hackers infiltrated federal ministries, Russian group sus-pected," [Online]. Available: http://www.dw.com/en/germany-admits-hackers-infiltrated-federa l-ministries-russian-group-suspected/a-42775517

Federal Office for Information Security, "Alliance for Cybersicherheit. General Information.," 01 08 2014. [Online]. Available: https://www.allianz-fuer-cybersicherheit.de/ACS/DE/_/download s/ACS_Broschuere_en.html?nn=6644222. Accessed 06 03 2018

Freiberg M (2016) Öffentlich-private Zusammenarbeit zum Schutz von IT-Infrastrukturen, in Cyber-sicherheit, Wiesbaden, Springer VS, pp 103–120

Fremuth M (2014) Wächst zusammen, was zusammengehört? Das Trennungsgebot zwischen Polizeibehörden und Nachrichtendiensten im Lichte der Reform der deutschen Sicherheitsbe-hörden., *AöR*, vol 139, pp 32–79

German Competence Centre against Cyber Crime, [Online]. Available: http://www.g4c-ev.org/. Accessed 06 March 2018

Gesetz über den Verfassungsschutz in Nordrhein-Westfalen (Verfassungsschutzgesetz Nordrhein-Westfalen - VSG NW -) vom 20.12.1994, zuletzt geändert durch Gesetz vom 20. September 2016, *GV.NRW*, p 789, 2016

Gesetz über die Errichtung des Bundesamtes für Sicherheit in der Informationstechnik vom 17. Dezember 1990, *BGBl. I*, p 2834, (1990)

Goetz J, Leyendecker H (2014) Rechnungsprüfer halten Cyber-Abwehrzentrum für "nicht gerechtfertigt". Süddeutsche Zeitung 07 Jun 2014. [Online] Available: http://www.sueddeutsche.de/dig ital/behoerde-in-bonn-rechnungspruefer-halten-cyber-abwehrzentrum-fuer-nicht-gerechtfertigt-1.1989433. Accessed 20 Jun 2018

Graulich K (2016) Elemente der sogenannten Neuen Sicherheitsarchitektur der Bundesrepublik. In: *Festgabe für Rosemarie Will 'Worüber reden wir eigentlich?'*, Berlin, pp 738–779

Hegele Y, Behnke N (2017) Horizontal coordination in cooperative federalism: the purpose of ministerial conferences in Germany. Reg Fed Stud 5:529–548

Innenministerium Niedersachsen (2011) AV Schwerpunktstaatsanwaltschaften zur Bekämpfung der Kriminalität im Zusammenhang mit Informations- und Kommunikationstechnik (IuK-Kriminalität) vom 04.11.2011, *Nds. MBl.*, no 43, p 834

Innenministerkonferenz (2017) "Sammlung der freigegebenen Beschlüsse der Innenministerkonferenz am 07./08.12.2017 in Leipzig," August 12 2017. [Online]. Available: https://www.in nenministerkonferenz.de/IMK/DE/termine/to-beschluesse/2017-12-07_08/beschluesse.pdf;jse ssionid=B48A17311B512333542F22CB2BBDFA56.1_cid382?__blob=publicationFile&v=3. Accessed 06 March 2018

Karl W, Soigne M (2017) Neue Rechtsgrundlagen für die Ausland-Ausland-Fernmeldeaufklärung, *NJW*, pp 919–925

Landesamt für Sicherheit in der Informationstechnik, "Aufgaben des LSI," [Online]. Available: https://www.lsi.bayern.de/lsi/index.html. Accessed 06 March 2018

Linke T (2015) Rechtsfragen der Einrichtung und des Betriebs eine Nationalen Cyber-Abwehrzentrums als informelle institutionalisierte Sicherheitskooperation, *Die Öffentliche Verwaltung*, pp 128–139

Marxsen C (2017) Verfassungsrechtliche Regeln für Cyberoperationen der Bundeswehr, *JZ*, no 11, pp 543–552

Schallbruch M (2017a) IT-Sicherheitsrecht – Schutz kritischer Infrastrukturen und staatlicher IT-Systeme. Zur Entwicklung des IT-Sicherheitsrechts in der 18. Wahlperiode (Teil 1), *CR*, pp 648–656

Schallbruch M (2017b) IT-Sicherheitsrecht – Schutz digitaler Dienste, Datenschutz und Datensicherheit, Zur Entwicklung des IT-Sicherheitsrechts in der 18. Wahlperiode (Teil 2), *CR*, pp 799–804

Schönbohm A (2011) Deutschlands Sicherheit: Cybercrime und Cyberwar, MV-Verlag

UP KRITIS-Geschäftsstelle (2017) "UP KRITIS-Jahresbericht 2017," 29 01 2018. [Online]. Available: https://www.kritis.bund.de/SharedDocs/Downloads/Kritis/DE/Jahresbericht_2017. pdf. Accessed 06 March 2018

Zedler D (2017) Zur strategischen Planung von cyber security in Deutschland. *Zeitschrift für Außen- und Sicherheitspolitik* 10:67–85

Chapter 5
Current Priorities and Gaps in German National Cybersecurity, Future Trends

Abstract Current German cybersecurity policy suffers from several gaps that this section examines in more detail. These gaps become apparent in international comparison and contrast with German officials' own claims that Germany's cybersecurity policy is strategically comprehensive. First, Germany has not devised a clear concept for the goal, scope, and legal framework of "active cyber defence" measures. Second, a major question remains that of the overarching institutional architecture for cybersecurity, including the responsibilities of the individual security authorities in the cyber domain and their differentiation and cooperation. Third, the debate on how the state should deal with IT security vulnerabilities is still in its infancy. Fourth, an implementation concept for the politically undisputed increase in the liability of software manufacturers for vulnerabilities in their products is lacking. Fifth, a national and European industrial policy on cybersecurity, which is widely called for under the banner of "digital sovereignty", is still largely undefined. Finally, Germany must define and assume a more comprehensive role in international efforts to maintain peace and stability in cyberspace.

Keywords Active cyberdefence · Cybersecurity architecture · Vulnerabilities
Digital sovereignty · Manufacturer's liability

5.1 Introduction

German policy-makers still understand cybersecurity to be primarily a preventive task of technical and organizational protection of IT. The core issues of German cybersecurity policy are

- the development of secure technologies,
- the dissemination of technical know-how,
- the technical and organizational security of critical systems,
- the legal obligation to and enforcement of protective measures,
- the development of defensive capabilities and increased criminal prosecution in the field of cyber crime.

© The Author(s) 2018
M. Schallbruch and I. Skierka, *Cybersecurity in Germany*, SpringerBriefs in Cybersecurity, https://doi.org/10.1007/978-3-319-90014-8_5

This civilian and preventive approach combines various paths of development. The strong influence of data protection with its emphasis on the legal, technical and organizational protection of systems has extended to the field of cybersecurity. The influential role of the BSI and its development towards a de facto national cybersecurity authority has made the engineering-oriented approach to cybersecurity, which stresses the development and deployment of well-defined secure systems, the guiding principle of cybersecurity policy. Other domestic security agencies have not yet or only temporarily found a place in the "digitizing" national security architecture. Moreover, their overlapping responsibilities often lead to their engagement into turf wars and blockages. Only the Bundeswehr (German Armed Forces) has promoted a more comprehensive view of security in the "cyber" domain in its national strategy. However, due to the tight legal restrictions relating to the Bundeswehr's deployment and competencies, it also remains more focused on securing its own systems than on cyber defence at home and abroad.

Industry, private associations, and companies have largely not yet devised a consistent cybersecurity strategy. German IT security companies support the idea of strengthening their industry and IT products on the national or European level, following the loosely defined principle of "digital sovereignty". However, they lack an agenda or strategy to implement this approach. Most of the big successful internet companies originate in the US or Asia, exporting their IT security know-how and solutions to Europe.

National standalone approaches are not competitive on a broad scale. Only in the area of critical infrastructures has Germany found a consistent and consequent approach to obliging the deployment of national certified IT security products through a mix of legal obligations and public-private cooperation. This is also fully in line with the tradition of the aforementioned preventive, technical-organizational strategic approach.

In contrast to its own claim, but also in international comparison, current German cybersecurity policy has several gaps which the following section examines in more detail.

5.2 Legal, Technical and Practical Development of Active Cyber Defence

Active cyber defence (ACD) has not been among German security agencies' instruments for many years. To date, no concrete actions have followed from the 2011 national cybersecurity strategy's (NCSS's) announcement to create a "complete set of instruments for the defence against attacks in cyberspace" (Bundesministerium des Innern 2011, p. 12). Instead, cyber defence in Germany followed a civilian preventive approach. On an international level, the debate about more far-reaching cyber defence actions has been ongoing for many years. There is no generally accepted term for ACD. According to cybersecurity expert Lachow, "ACD can best be understood as a set of operating concepts that all involve taking the initiative and engaging the adversary in some way" (Lachow 2013, p. 3). ACD can comprise a set of measures which the defender uses in its own IT systems, such as the redirection of traffic or deception of the attacker. Yet, ACD can also affect provider networks, through measures such as the setting up of sinkholes for data flows. It can affect third-party systems if the attacked party manipulates an attack's Command & Control (C2) servers. Finally, ACD can also involve action in the attacker's systems, including the manipulation of attack tools or deletion of data. Tactically, each of these options can make sense at certain stages of a cyber attack (Lachow 2013, p. 1). However, the deployment of such tactics can raise legal concerns, increase operational risks (such as detection) or cause collateral damage. The latter could, for instance, occur in the form of political or diplomatic disruptions if a defending party's measures compromised servers in other countries (Reinhold and Schulze 2017).

There are a number of scenarios in which such measures seem necessary. This could be, for example, the takedown of a botnet. The US Federal Bureau of Investigation (FBI), in cooperation with private sector partners, regularly engages in botnet takedowns. Germany has benefited from such operations without executing takedowns itself. A takedown could involve the destruction of leaked data on drop zone servers. It could also include the disruption of C2 servers that control physical attacks, such as detonating bombs (Reinhold and Schulze 2017, p. 6).

Germany's government has not yet developed a legal framework for ACD actions and has no authority for far-reaching active cyber operations. ACD activities in Germany have thus to date been limited to operations carried out in cooperation with the respective providers or system operators, and in cross-border operations by means of international legal assistance. The debate on active cyber operations in reaction to attacks did not begin until 2017. Back then, the Federal Minister of the Interior announced a corresponding concept, the Federal Security Council (Bundessicherheitsrat) is said to have addressed the issue in a secret meeting (Reinhold and Schulze 2017, p. 3), and various federal agencies offered to expand their scope of activities accordingly (Tanriverdi 2017a, b). In Germany, the discussion about ACD is taking place under the buzzword "Hack-Back"; however, this refers to the complete spectrum of active cyber operations, not only to the infiltration of adversarial systems to defend against an ongoing cyber attack (responsive cyber defence).

While Germany continues to approach ACD measures only cautiously, cyber operations in the form of "lawful hacking" for criminal prosecution purposes have found their way into the competencies and capability development of the security agencies. This is mainly due to the increasing undermining of a key investigative tool, notably lawful interception. Due to the increase in the encryption of communications and the use of unmonitorable services such as "The Onion Router" or Tor software ("going dark"), security agencies need to find ways to access electronic communications directly on the suspect's systems.

In 2006, the parliament of North Rhine-Westphalia gave the State Office for the Protection of the Constitution the authority to secretly penetrate computer systems in order to monitor suspects. The respective law was overturned by the Federal Constitutional Court (Bundesverfassungsgericht 2008; Hornung 2008).

Later, however, the law of a number of Länder regulated this power for state intelligence services and the Federal Criminal Police. Ultimately, covert access to computers was allowed for law enforcement agencies in the summer of 2017 but limited to the prosecution of particularly serious crimes (Singelnstein and Derin 2017). Government hacking for purposes of law enforcement and for certain limited intelligence purposes is successively being introduced into German security policy—and is being discussed critically, especially with regard to the handling of vulnerabilities (Herpig 2017). In order to support police forces and intelligence services in the development of relevant methods, a new authority was established in 2017, the Central Office for Information Technology in the Security Sphere (Zentrale Stelle für Informationstechnik im Sicherheitsbereich, ZITiS). It is supervised by the Interior Ministry. Its task is to develop techniques for lawful interception, online searches, cryptoanalysis, digital forensics and big data analyses (Bundesministerium des Innern 2016, p. 32).

It remains to be seen how these different singular approaches of active cyber and legal hacking operations will be combined into an overall strategy. Substantial legal, technical and organisational questions remain. From a legal point of view, it is not clear whether ACD will be implemented successively as an extension of the competencies of the various security agencies, intelligence services, police forces and the BSI, or whether a holistic approach will be found. The latter seems to make sense for two reasons. First, ACD, which affects the rights of third parties, is accompanied by a significant risk of collateral damage, which has to be considered holistically. Second, all actions that have an impact outside Germany are relevant to foreign policy; their legal regulation must provide for a foreign policy cross-check, including the involvement of the Foreign Ministry. In any case, a legal regulation also requires a graduated list of measures and an increasingly strict obligation to observe a duty of care depending on the balancing of the purpose and the respective rights of third parties.

From a technical point of view, the question is how the tools for ACD are developed, who is in charge of assessing them and how they are deployed in order to minimise collateral damage. ZITiS will have an important role to play here. In addition, the involvement of internet providers in defence efforts must be even more intensive than before. Finally, it is also necessary to answer the organisational question relating to which institution shall be responsible for active cyber defence. This must be answered in the context of the cybersecurity architecture as a whole, which we will come to in the following section.

5.3   Cybersecurity Architecture—Roles and Responsibilities of Agencies

German security agencies operate in absence of an overarching cybersecurity architecture. Cybersecurity responsibilities have progressively increased for almost all security agencies and several other authorities. The only significant organizational developments in the German cybersecurity landscape are the continuous strengthening of the BSI with new tasks and new personnel, the concentration of the military's capabilities in the CIR command, as well as the establishment of central units at the state level, mainly in the police force and sometimes in the intelligence service. None of these steps have solved any of the four structural problems facing the German security apparatus in cyberspace.

First, there is no clear *responsibility for cyber defence at the federal level*. The cyber defence centre operates only to a very limited extent, the Bundeswehr is not responsible, and the BSI is working considerably above its capacity. A fundamental reorganization is necessary here by creating a cyber defence authority with clear responsibility. Second, the widening of *active cyber defence requires a defined competence* at the federal level. In priniciple, the BSI has the necessary capabilities. However, it should be excluded as a responsible authority because active operations do not suit the character of the agency's preventive security mission. The domestic intelligence services and the police are limited to domestic activities, which means that only the Bundeswehr or the BND can carry out such operations. The decision is a political and legal question. If Germany wants to remain in line with its defensive approach, the military should be excluded. Military cyber defence operations tend to escalate conflicts. In addition, the Bundeswehr's powers under constitutional law are far more limited than those of the Foreign Intelligence Service BND.

To combine the two issues—cyber defence in Germany and the execution of active operations that can also affect foreign countries—it would be reasonable to create a new institution, a cyber defence agency that is responsible for the recognition, analysis and holistic defence of attacks with the help of the police and intelligence services in Germany and the help of the BND abroad. The military would need to be involved as well. The BSI, on the other hand, would only participate in this process insofar as insights from ongoing attacks are relevant for the establishment of protective measures by the government or critical infrastructures. In any case, a comprehensive and extensively debated amendment of the law is a prerequisite for a proper distribution of responsibilities.

The third structural problem is the *link with the Länder*. Even if under the German constitutional order, domestic security is first of all a matter for the federal states, there is no resistance to a strong federal approach to cyber defence among the Länder interior ministers. Creating cyber defence authorities 16 times over across the federal states is impossible due to the international nature of cyber defence, its closeness to military defence and the expense of developing human and technical resources. Given that the federal states are nevertheless responsible for police and intelligence services, a central institution of each of the Länder must be closely linked to the federal cyber defence agency, ideally a central unit of the state police. Local police powers, e.g. to conduct home searches or shutdown of servers, may be required for cyber defence purposes.

Finally, a fourth structural problem still needs to be solved, the *cooperation between security agencies and the private sector*. Germany needs to create a cybersecurity operations platform that is as uniform as possible between the government and the private sector. The very inconsistent manner in which security-relevant information is exchanged between public sector authorities and companies today is not acceptable in the long term. The government cannot justify the fact that it is largely coincidental as to whether or not information that is necessary for a company's self-protection reaches it. There are many reasons why the BSI should establish such a central platform for all federal authorities, including intelligence services, police forces and a cyber defence agency. Technical parameters are at the core of an operational information exchange. Intelligence findings or police information may only be shared with third parties to a very limited extent, so that they are not suitable for a platform. The government might require the industry to become more concentrated, for example, through a joint private sector institution that brings together industries and companies with the BSI platform.

It remains to be seen whether the new federal government, which came into office in the spring of 2018, will tackle such a major structural reform of the cybersecurity architecture in Germany.

5.4 Towards a Governmental Vulnerability Handling Strategy

The increased use of encryption in communication tools and web services poses a growing challenge for law enforcement agencies (LEAs) all over the world. LEAs argue they are at risk of criminals "going dark" due to the LEAs' inability to investigate criminal suspects' encrypted communication. Several countries, such as the United Kingdom, France, or the US, have adopted or are debating laws to give authorities the right to interfere with cryptography. In contrast, the German federal government has so far abstained from options to weaken cryptographic security mechanisms and instead adhered to the "principles of cryptography", which the Cabinet established in 1999. At the core of these principles lies the government's commitment to never ban or weaken crypto products (Bundesregierung 1999). Indeed, the installation of backdoors into crypto products would undermine the security of IT and thereby, of its users, and would severely impair confidence in German technology products on the global market, in turn harming the German IT industry.

Therefore, Germany aims to strengthen LEAs' and intelligence agencies' capabilities to circumvent encryption through "advanced technical procedures." In this context, Germany established the aforementioned Central Authority for Information Technology in the Security Sphere (ZITiS). As pointed out above, one of its tasks is to develop tools and capacities for government hacking to gain targeted access to computer systems, interception of communication, and analysis.

Government hacking often relies on the exploitation of a vulnerability—a flaw in software or hardware which enables third parties to gain access to a system directly or via an "exploit". Vulnerabilities might be known to the manufacturer (for n number of days, therefore referred to as "n-days") or unknown to the manufacturer (for 0 days, therefore referred to as "0-days"). Once a third party, for example, a security researcher, discloses an 0-day to the manufacturer, the manufacturer can develop and deploy a patch which fixes the vulnerability. In general, most IT products contain a multitude of vulnerabilities, especially as the majority of IT systems become increasingly complex.

At the time of writing, the rules for government hacking in Germany are far from settled and fiercely debated (Krempl 2017; Herpig 2017). Most importantly, it is unclear how security agencies will handle vulnerabilities in IT systems, which they inevitably need to exploit for their (targeted) surveillance activities. If government agencies exploit 0-day vulnerabilities in IT products without disclosing them to the products' manufacturers, the vulnerabilities will likely not receive a patch and therefore remain open for any motivated and capable malicious actor to exploit. Hence, such use of undiscovered vulnerabilities by state security agencies bears risks for the overall IT-ecosystem and society at large.

This is one reason why the German (and global) IT industry and civil society organizations resist government hacking efforts. Moreover, the exploitation of vulnerabilities in IT security products interferes with individuals' legally-guaranteed rights to the protection of the integrity and confidentiality of IT systems enshrined in a 2008 German Constitutional Court ruling (Abel and Schafer 2009). Therefore, the intrusion of security agencies into computer systems via the exploitation of an unknown vulnerability requires appropriate and proportionate justification within the remits of the national criminal and basic law.

The CDU/CSU and SPD governing coalition will need to address a number of political, ethical, and legal challenges related to the handling of IT security vulnerabilities. The otherwise comprehensive set of cybersecurity measures outlined in the government's coalition treaty from 2018 did not include any reference to government agencies' handling of IT security vulnerabilities (CDU/CSU and SPD 2018). Within the 19th legislative period which began in 2018, the government will need to devise a process or set of rules and parameters guiding security agencies' legal and legitimate exploitation of IT vulnerabilities.

One option would be to authorize security agencies to use known n-day vulnerabilities only. In fact, many systems remain unpatched even after vulnerabilities are known. The annual Verizon Data Breach Investigation Report has regularly concluded that most attacks against IT systems exploited well-known vulnerabilities for which patches had long been available (Verizon 2015, 2017). Hence, there are chances that security agencies could still gain access to a system via known vulnerabilities. From an IT security perspective, this is a practicable and preferable solution. However, prosecutors argue that they need 0-day vulnerabilities to stay one step ahead of sophisticated criminals.

In this context, another option would be to authorize security agencies to exploit 0-day vulnerabilities, which bears significant and potentially systemic security risks. For example, the exploitation of a previously unknown vulnerability in a widely used operating system, such as Microsoft Windows, could have dramatic consequences worldwide. Accordingly, first ideas and procedures to assess possible consequences of the use of vulnerabilities by security agencies in the context of potential gains for security agencies are emerging. The US has adopted an interagency "Vulnerabilities Equities Process" in which different government stakeholders assess the tradeoff between the national security benefits of using an 0-day vulnerability and the security risks it poses to critical infrastructures and IT systems generally, were the vulnerability to be exploited by malicious actors (Government of the United States 2017).

The US Vulnerabilities Equities Process might provide some guidance for the Germany, for example when it comes to the inclusion of multiple stakeholders with different interests. However, as (Gaycken 2017) points out, the decision-making within such a process risks becoming a political negotiation subject to power dynamics among different government departments and stakeholders. While such dynamics can never be avoided in practice, a vulnerability equities process should follow clearly defined criteria and ensure a balance between stakeholders. The assessment should weigh the criticality of a vulnerability for individual users and systemic security of IT against the value of this vulnerability for solving crimes or national security (Gaycken 2017). Following a precautionary approach, vulnerabilities that would have a very serious impact on human life or the economy if exploited by criminal actors should always be disclosed to the technology's manufacturer. Above all, an equity process needs to be based on a clear legal basis, follow a transparent legislative procedure, and happen under judicial oversight, none of which exists to date in Germany. While the IT industry, representatives from the judiciary, and civil society representatives cannot participate in case-by-case decision processes, the government should institute a regular dialogue about the handling of vulnerabilities with them. Moreover, the IT industry itself should transparently document their own handling of vulnerabilities in their products and support users with fixing them.

Overall, the German government will need to address the handling of both known and unknown vulnerabilities within a comprehensive set of considerations, including the cyber threat situation, the diversity or monoculture of hard- and software deployed in systems at home and abroad, and alternative ways to gain access to information within a criminal prosecution.

5.5 Implementing a Comprehensive IT Security Industry Policy

One of the guiding themes of German cybersecurity strategy has been the strengthening of the German and European IT industry, with a focus on trustworthy and secure ICT products. The most recent 2016 national cybersecurity strategy (NCSS) outlines the goal to better promote the development of key technologies and quality IT "made in Germany".

Indeed, the deployment of reliable and trustworthy IT components in critical infrastructures, industry, and individual user environments is a key enabler for cybersecurity. Following the Snowden revelations, political and industry leaders in Germany and Europe called for regaining the country's and region's "technological sovereignty", including industrial policy measures to strengthen the domestic IT industry and to reduce the dependence on foreign IT components, which might contain backdoors (Gallagher 2014).

However, as the European Network and Information Security Agency (ENISA) pointed out in 2014, "over the past 15 years Europe has lost its leading position in ICT technology. All the new global players are situated outside the EU" (ENISA 2014). The most recent German Ministry of Economics and Energy's report on the IT security market in Germany dating from 2014 shows that domestic demand in Germany for IT security products[1] has been met by around 22% of imported and the remaining share of 78% by domestic products (Bundesministerium für Wirtschaft und Energie 2014). Hence, the German IT security industry, including IT services, software, and hardware, is meeting high domestic demand but its exports remain low compared to US or Chinese ICT products. Moreover, while the share of software of the German IT security market has increased to 44%, the share of hardware has decreased to only 4% (from 13% in 2005) in 2013. One reason for this trend might be the growing importance of software in increasingly interconnected environments and the "Internet of Things" (IoT) (KPMG 2014).

In the field of critical infrastructures, Germany has succeeded to implement legal and technical measures obliging operators and technology manufacturers to comply with specific industrial and regulatory IT security standards (Schallbruch 2017a). However, across the broader industrial context, measures that promote the deployment of trustworthy IT are still outstanding. A number of industry and government-commissioned studies have examined means to enhance Germany's, the industry's or individuals' ability of self-determined and autonomous action in the digital realm through secure and trustworthy ICTs (Forschungszentrum Informatik et al. 2017; Diekmann 2015). Proposed measures include the expansion and enhancement of national key technologies, an increase of investment in research and development, the enforcement of technical guidelines and standards as part of a European certification scheme (see Sect. 5.5), leveraging the EU's public procurement mechanisms, the promotion of innovative business sectors and models, and mechanisms to improve the education of technology and IT experts (Forschungszentrum Informatik et al. 2017; Diekmann 2015; KPMG 2014).

The lack of a comprehensive national and a properly coordinated EU industry policy for the IT (security) sector constitutes a significant gap in German and European digital policy. While national investment as well as research and development programs will help promote national industrial initiatives, an internationally competitive IT industry will likely be able to emerge only at the European level. The German government will be well-advised to cooperate with its European partners, and France in particular, to promote innovative business models for EU companies producing IT and cybersecurity products and services—moving toward an IT "made in Europe" rather than a "made in Germany" approach.

First steps can be recognized in the current government's 2018 coalition treaty, which announces the establishment of a public Franco-German centre for artificial

---

[1]The share of the IT security industry of the total ICT industry in Germany is around 10%.

intelligence. Moreover, the treaty declares to establish a strategic industry and inno-vation policy to support the expansion of Industry 4.0 (CDU/CSU and SPD 2018, p. 13). It aims to promote, in a targeted manner, digital key technologies, as well as the investment into research and development efforts to advance key technologies such as microelectronics, quantum computing, robotics, Blockchain, and others, and to continue to invest in microelectronic technologies (CDU/CSU and SPD 2018, p. 57).

Germany should assign priority to implement such suggestions and avoid being left behind by other countries, including France, which has adopted an ambitious digital agenda under President Emmanuel Macron. Overall, the promotion of indus-trial and societal cybersecurity should be seen as part of a broader future-driven technology policy strategy which requires cooperation with European partners, the promotion of high security and reliability standards, and foundations to enable Euro-pean companies to innovate.

5.6 Finding a Coherent Legal Concept for Safety and Security

In the relatively short period between 2013 and 2017, the German government passed numerous laws on IT security. In addition, there are important provisions of European law which have become directly applicable in Germany or have been transposed into national law, such as the NIS Directive, the eIDAS regulation or the GDPR (Schallbruch 2017a). At the heart of the regulations are requirements for various types of operators of IT systems and providers of digital services to apply preventive IT security measures and report security incidents to the authorities. Corresponding obligations exist for operators of critical infrastructures (Hornung 2015; Schallbruch 2017a), web server operators (Gerlach 2015), providers of significant digital services such as online marketplaces, search engines, and cloud services (Schallbruch 2017b), and, in accordance with Art. 32 of the new GDPR, also for operators of systems on which personal data are processed (Schallbruch 2017b).

Although the requirements of the different legal areas differ considerably in detail, the final result is that the operators or providers must implement state-of-the-art IT security measures.

Germany has failed to achieve the politically intended tightening of the liability of IT manufacturers for the security of their products. In the common opinion of German scholars, the provisions of existing law are not sufficient to force manufacturers to maintain a minimum level of security and to act responsibly when dealing with warnings, vulnerabilities, patches and updates (Spindler 2016). Whereas there is no suitable manufacturer responsibility for the IT products that are available on the market in Germany, a large number of special categories of products are precisely specified by government specifications as to which security measures must be taken for products. This concerns for example medical devices, smart energy meters or IT components in the infrastructure of health care. They require state approval on the basis of defined IT security standards, which are usually developed by the BSI.

The consequence is an enormous differentiation in the market for IT products. On the one hand, there is a state-regulated sector with special German IT security requirements and correspondingly high-security products, and on the other hand there is a largely unregulated sector of IT products without any IT security requirements, i.e. consumer products. The new government, which took office in March 2018, wants to overhaul this state. The coalition agreement includes various statements on this issue. The aim is to establish minimum security standards for consumer-related products and to establish duties of care for manufacturers, such as the prompt identification and elimination of vulnerabilities. Manufacturer liability is also to be increased (CDU/CSU and SPD 2018, pp. 45, 128).

This approach is significantly different from the current considerations at the European level. For this purpose, the European Commission presented comprehensive proposals in September 2017 (European Commission 2017). The existing national certification procedures are to be gradually replaced by a European framework. The Commission itself intends to be empowered to make certification schemes binding for product groups on the basis of preliminary work. The present draft regulation does not provide for the content of such a certification but leaves it to the individual schemes. If a European cybersecurity certification scheme has been defined for a product group, the member states should be prevented from defining their own schemes for this product group. At the same time, the Commission wants to be able to use its implementing act to determine whether the existing national schemes lose their validity at a given time. In this way, a European regime could gradually replace national rules.

The certification itself would be executed by certification and accreditation bodies established by national law. Certificates shall be completely voluntary. Each company could then decide whether and where to apply for a European Cybersecurity Certificate. Certificates issued shall be valid for three years. The Commission proposes three different security levels (basic, substantial, high) without specifying exactly what these levels mean. This would also have to be determined on a product group-specific basis.

Overall, this proposal is a step in the right direction towards a uniform European assessment of the security of IT products. Nonetheless, the voluntary approach, which also ties in very strongly with traditional IT security certification, falls short of expectations. The Commission has not put forward any proposals on how the responsibility (and also liability) of manufacturers and service providers for the safety of their products can be increased. Their proposal does not even indicate how to overcome the current problems of safety certification—speed, cost, low "lifetime". The speed of the certification processes is significantly slower than the speed of technical innovation. The costs of the certification procedures, in particular the re-certification required for each change, are high. Due to changes in risks and attack vectors, certificates must be limited in time. Even if these problem were solved, the member states would hardly be able to accept a Commission-exclusive decision on the security requirements for ICT products.

It remains to be seen how the new German government's approach to tightening liability can be reconciled with the European approach of voluntary certification.

5.7 International Cooperation

Collaboration with other states and non-state actors at the international level is key to the advancement of Germany's and indeed any country's interests in the field of cybersecurity, relating to technical IT security, critical infrastructure protection, counter cyber crime and espionage, or national defence. The very basis of the Internet is globalized, and so are the organizations and companies that constitute and administer it (Hathaway and Klimburg 2012, p. 30).

International diplomatic cooperation is a crucial means to prevent and manage interstate conflict in the digital realm in the absence of binding international legal rules. Cooperation can occur through internationally binding treaties, politically binding agreements, such as confidence building measures, as well as nongovernmental agreements between technical bodies (Hathaway and Klimburg 2012).

In light of growing political tensions between major powers such as the United States (US), Russia, and China, it is crucial that the German government, together with like-minded European and international partners, takes a leading role in reinvigorating an inclusive international effort to maintain peace and stability in cyberspace. Since the emergence of the first IT security and critical infrastructure protection policies at the national level in the 1990s, the German government coordinated its efforts with the United States and other European Union (EU) member states. Throughout the past decade, Germany has assumed an active role in international cyber diplomacy as well as internet governance.

Cyber diplomacy can be understood as the general formal state engagement of a nation's diplomatic processes in the overall theme of global cybersecurity (Potter 2002; Luiijf and Healey 2012). In particular, cyber diplomacy refers to multilateral or bilateral activity to manage interstate relationships in cyberspace, for example within the United Nations (UN). Internet governance, on the other hand, can loosely be defined as the decentralized, bottom-up policies and mechanisms under which the Internet community's many stakeholders—technical organizations such as the Internet Engineering Task Force (IETF) or the Internet Corporation of Assigned Names and Numbers (ICANN), private companies, civil society, academia, and governments—make decisions about the development and use of the Internet (Masters 2014). [The World Summit on the Information Society's official definition can be found in (World Summit on the Information Society 2005)]. In this context, governments cooperate with various non-state stakeholders. Since 2005, stakeholders convene at the global UN Internet Governance Forum (IGF) on an annual basis to discuss all internet governance related issues.

As previously discussed, Germany has participated in negotiations on cybersecurity within the UN since 2004, as well as in other bilateral and multilateral formats. However, most of its international cooperation was limited to technical exchange. While the first national cybersecurity strategy in 2011 mentioned the international and diplomatic dimensions of cybersecurity policy, it was not until the Snowden revelations that Germany started to play a greater role on the international stage. In response to the revelations, which included details about the surveillance of German Chancellor Angela Merkel and Brazilian President Dilma Rousseff, Germany and Brazil sponsored a UN resolution that called on states to "respect and protect the right to privacy" in the digital age. On December 18, 2013, the UN General Assembly adopted the final resolution 68/167 (United Nations General Assembly 2014). Thereby, Germany and Brazil assumed a leading role in efforts to enshrining the right to privacy online in international norms and law. Despite subsequent revelations exposing German intelligence agencies' close cooperation with the NSA and the British GCHQ, the resolution remains a major diplomatic achievement for Germany. It is also noteworthy that Germany partnered with an ally outside of its European and transatlantic ties, which made it a more global effort.

In the following years, Germany has continued to be an active promoter of cyber diplomacy. Under German chairmanship in 2016, the Organization for Cooperation and Security in Europe's (OSCE) adopted a second package of confidence building measures (CBMs) in cyberspace (Organization for Security and Co-operation in Europe 2016). Moreover, its diplomatic representatives chaired the latest UN Group of Governmental Experts on Information Security (GGE) from 2016 to 2017. The UN GGE group had convened for five rounds since 2004 to address threats of armed conflict in cyberspace and drafted principles for norms and standards of responsible state behavior. In 2013, the group issued a landmark report in which 15 countries, including Russia, China, the US, India, the UK, France and Germany, agreed that "international law, and in particular the Charter of the United Nations, is applicable and is essential to maintaining peace and stability and promoting an open, secure peaceful and accessible ICT environment" (United Nations General Assembly 2013). A subsequent report in 2015 endorsed new norms to guide state activity in cyberspace during peacetime. This included the norms that states should refrain from targeting each other's critical infrastructure, that they should not target other states' authorized computer emergency response teams, known as "CERTs" or "CSIRTs", and that they should not knowingly let their territory be used for internationally wrongful acts using cyberspace (United Nations General Assembly 2015). Germany chaired the fifth iteration of the group, which was tasked with discussing the application of the laws of war to an online conflict. Yet, in summer 2017, the process to write the rules that should guide state activity in cyberspace came to a halt. The GGE talks collapsed without a consensus report due to fundamental divides between a coalition of Western states on the one side and Russia, China and others, on the other. As (Grigsby 2017) points out, a major problem was that the UN diplomatic efforts "looked increasingly divorced from the operational reality of state-sponsored cyber actions". Indeed, state-sponsored malicious cyber activities have intensified throughout the past years. For example, the US and Israel allegedly launched a covert operation called "Olympic Games" in 2008 which targeted Iranian nuclear facilities, and Russian state-sponsored hackers are suspected of having been responsible for cyber attacks that caused power outages in Ukraine in 2015 and 2016, as well as attempting to influence democratic elections in other states through the use of hacking and online disinformation campaigns.

Other efforts to defend cyber-norms processes such as the EU's adoption of a "cyber toolbox", which enables the EU to levy sanctions in response to a state-sponsored cyber evidence, constitutes an important diplomatic initiative, but does not present a set of rules that are shared by states such as Russia or China (Grigsby 2017).

With ever deepening divides among major powers over cybersecurity and international security more generally, Germany should cooperate with France as well as other European and international partners to develop a model code of good governance in cyberspace. The code should promote a free and secure cyberspace and include clear rejections of human rights violations online and propaganda manipulations of democratic processes (Schallbruch, Gaycken and Skierka 2018). Germany should specifically also look to rising non-Western democratic powers for cooperation, such as in the context of the UN resolution on the right to digital privacy in 2014 when it had partnered with Brazil. Moreover, to achieve an overarching acceptance, Germany could include non-state actors into these efforts.

In order to strengthen Germany's international role in cybersecurity and good governance of the internet, the government should specifically strengthen the German federal foreign office's role in national as well as international cybersecurity policy and equip it with personnel and organizational additional resources. In 2019, Germany will host the UN Internet Governance Forum (IGF) in Berlin, which presents an additional opportunity for Germany to assume a leading role.

References

Abel W, Schafer B (2009) The German constitutional court on the right in confidentiality and integrity of information technology systems—a case report on BVerfG, NJW 2008, 822. SCRIPT 6(1):106–123

Bundesministerium des Innern (2011) Cyber-Sicherheitsstrategie für Deutschland. Berlin

Bundesministerium des Innern (2016) Cyber-Sicherheitsstrategie für Deutschland. Berlin

Bundesministerium für Wirtschaft und Energie (2014) Der IT-Sicherheitsmarkt in Deutschland. Berlin

Bundesregierung (1999) Bericht der Bundesregierung zu den Auswirkungen der Nutzung kryptografischer Verfahren auf die Arbeit der Strafverfolgungs- und Sicherheitsbehörden (Ziffer 4 der Eckpunkte der deutschen Kryptopolitik vom 2. Juni 1999) "Verschlüsselungsbericht"

Bundesverfassungsgericht (2008) NJW. p 822

CDU/CSU, SPD (2018) Ein neuer Aufbruch für Europa. Eine neue Dynamik für Deutschland. Ein neuer Zusammenhalt für unser Land. Koalitionsvertrag zwischen CDU/CSU und SPD, vol 19. Legislaturperiode, Berlin

Diekmann G (2015) Digitale Souveränität - Positionsbestimmung und erste Handlungsempfehlungen für Deutschland und Europa. Bitkom, Berlin

ENISA (2014) Europe's ICT sector—the need for coordinated and responsive EU policies (July 2014) [online]. Available: https://www.enisa.europa.eu/events/enisa-events/enisa-high-level-event-2014-and-ecsm-launch/eu-digital-security-policy Accessed: 20 Jun 2018

European Commission (2017) Title III of the Proposal for a Regulation on ENISA, the "EU Cybersecurity Agency", and repealing Regulation (EU) 526/2013, and on Information and Communication Technology cybersecurity certification ("Cybersecurity Act"), 2017-09-13, COM (2017) 477 final

Forschungszentrum Informatik, Accenture GmbH, Bitkom Research GmbH (2017) "Kompetenzen für eine Digitale Souveränität," Bundesministerium für Wirtschaft und Energie (BMWi)

Gallagher S (2014) Photos of an NSA "upgrade" factory show Cisco router getting implant. Ars Technica (14 May 2014) [Online]. Available: https://arstechnica.com/tech-policy/2014/05/photo s-of-an nsa upgrade-factory-show-cisco-router-getting-implant/. Accessed 31 Mar 2018

Gaycken S (2017) Recommendations for the development of vulnerability equities processes In: DSI industrial and policy recommendations, vol 7

Gerlach C (2015) Sicherheitsanforderungen für Telemediendienste – der neue § 13 Abs. 7 TMG. CR, p 581

Government of the United States (2017) Vulnerabilities equities policy and process for the United States Government

Grigsby A (2017) The end of cyber norms. Survival 59(6):109–122

Hathaway M, Klimburg A (2012) Preliminary considerations: on national cyber security. In: National cyber security framework manual, NATO Cooperative Cyber Defence Centre of Excellence, Tallinn, pp 1–43

Herpig S (2017) Government hacking. Global challenges. Stiftung Neue Verantwortung Impulse, Oct 2017, pp 1–18

Hornung G (2008) Ein neues Grundrecht. Kommentierung zur BVerfG-Entscheidung. CR, p 299

Hornung G (2015) Neue Pflichten für Betreiber kritischer Infrastrukturen: Das IT-Sicherheitsgesetz des Bundes. NJW, p 3334

KPMG (2014) IT-Sicherheit in Deutschland - Handlungsempfehlungen für eine zielorientierte Umsetzung des IT-Sicherheitsgesetztes

Krempl S (2017) Staatstrojaner-Gesetz: Nächster Halt Bundesverfassungsgericht, Heise online (23 June 2017) [Online]. Available https://www.heise.de/newsticker/meldung/Staatstrojaner-Gesetz-Naechster-Halt-Bundesverfassungsgericht-3754891.html, Accessed 31 Mar 2018

Lachow I (2013) Active cyber defense: a framework for policymakers. Center for New American Security Policy Brief (Feb 2013)

Luiijf E, Healey J (2012) Organisational structures & considerations. In: National cyber security framework manual, NATO CCDCOE, Tallinn, pp 108–145

Masters J (2014) What is internet governance? Council on foreign relations (23 Apr 2014) [Online]. Available: https://www.cfr.org/backgrounder/what-internet-governance. Accessed 31 Mar 2018

Organization for Security and Co-operation in Europe (2016) Decision No. 1202—OSCE confidence-building measures to reduce the risks of conflict stemming from the use of information and communication technologies

Potter EH (2002) Cyber-diplomacy: managing foreign policy in the twenty-first century. McGill-Queen's University Press, Quebec

Reinhold T, Schulze M (2017) Digitale Gegenangriffe. Eine Analyse der technischen und politischen Implikationen von "hack backs", vol 1. Arbeitspapier der Stiftung Wissenschaft und Politik

Schallbruch M (2017a) IT-Sicherheitsrecht – Schutz kritischer Infrastrukturen und staatlicher IT-Systeme. Zur Entwicklung des IT-Sicherheitsrechts in der 18. Wahlperiode (Teil 1). CR 648–656

Schallbruch M (2017b) IT-Sicherheitsrecht – Schutz digitaler Dienste, Datenschutz und Datensicherheit. Zur Entwicklung des IT-Sicherheitsrechts in der 18. Wahlperiode (Teil 2) CR 799–804

Schallbruch M, Gaycken S, Skierka I (2018) Cybersicherheit 2018–2020: Handlungsvorschläge für CDU/CSU und SPD. DSI Industry & Policy Recommendations (IPR) Series, vol 1

Singelnstein T, Derin B (2017) Das Gesetz zur effektiveren und praxistauglicheren Ausgestaltung des Strafverfahrens NJW, p 2646

Spindler G (2016) IT-Sicherheitsgesetz und zivilrechtliche Haftung. CR 297

Tanriverdi H (2017a) Der gefährliche Wunsch nach digitalen Gegenangriffen (10 Jan 2017) [Online]. Available: http://www.sueddeutsche.de/digital/verfassungsschutz-der-gefaehrliche-wu nsch-nach-digitalen-gegenangriffen-1.3327618. Accessed 07 Mar 2018

Tanriverdi H (2017b) Bundesbehörde diskutiert digitale Gegenschläge (21 June 2017) [Online]. Available: http://www.sueddeutsche.de/digital/it-sicherheit-bundesbehoerde-diskutiert-ob-sie-z urueck-hacken-soll-1.3554124. Accessed 07 Mar 2018

United Nations General Assembly (2013) Report of the group of governmental experts on develop-
    ments in the field of information and telecommunications in the context of international security,
    A/68/98
United Nations General Assembly (2014) Revised draft resolution on the right to privacy in the
    digital age
United Nations General Assembly (2015) Report of the group of governmental experts on develop-
    ments in the field of information and telecommunications in the context of international security,
    A/70/174
Verizon (2015) 2015 Data breach investigations report
Verizon (2017) 2017 Data breach investigations report, 10th edn
World Summit on the Information Society (2005) Tunis agenda for the information society

Chapter 6
Conclusion

Abstract With a strong defensive, technically and organizationally oriented approach, Germany has now achieved a high level of cybersecurity development. Following the US, Germany was one of the first countries with a far-reaching strategy to protect critical information infrastructures. Its implementation has been achieved through a mixture of a regulatory approach and a public-private partnership, and is well underway compared to other European countries. Germany has also made reasonably rapid progress in setting up and legally enforcing the fight against cyber crime. The country has had a strong influence on European strategy and regulation in these two areas, protecting critical infastructures and fighting cyber crime. Cybersecurity as an area of policy has attained high priority in Germany. The new federal government, formed in 2018, has recognized the need for a radical overhaul of the architecture of the German security agencies to meet the challenges of cybersecurity. However, it is doubtful whether the government will manage to restructure the complex distribution of responsibilities within the German state organisation. In any case, the further opening of the German cybersecurity policy towards more active cyber defence measures and the creation of corresponding legal regulations and practical facilities is likely. The central question of German politics will continue to be the right balance between ensuring cybersecurity and national security on the one hand and protecting civil liberties and privacy on the other. It would be a welcome development if the country, on the basis of these approaches, were to engage more strongly in the international debate.

Keyword Cybersecurity · National security · Civil liberties · Diplomacy

With a strong defensive, technically and organizationally oriented approach, Germany has now achieved a high level of cybersecurity development. Following the US, Germany was one of the first countries with a far-reaching strategy to protect critical information infrastructures. Its implementation has been achieved through a mixture of a regulatory approach and a public-private partnership and is well underway compared to other European countries. Germany has also made reasonably rapid progress in setting up and legally enforcing the fight against cyber crime. The country has had a strong influence on European strategy and regulation in these two areas,

© The Author(s) 2018

M. Schallbruch and I. Skierka, *Cybersecurity in Germany*, SpringerBriefs
in Cybersecurity, https://doi.org/10.1007/978-3-319-90014-8_6

protecting CI and fighting cyber crime. Especially the large businesses in Germany have supported the national strategy through active involvement in public-private partnerships, such as UP KRITIS, or through the establishment of industry joint ventures such as the German Cybersecurity Organization (DCSO).

Cybersecurity as an area of policy has become a very high priority in Germany—in government, industry and public perception. Until 2016, however, the overarching strategy remained very limited to CI protection and the fight against cyber crime. Since then, the focus has expanded. The Bundeswehr is more strongly concerned with international security and military aspects of cybersecurity. The technology policy discussion of cybersecurity is increasingly evolving from a purely political debate to an administrative strategy. The new federal government, formed in 2018, has recognized the need for a radical overhaul of the architecture of the German security agencies to meet the challenges of cybersecurity. However, it is doubtful whether the government will manage to restructure the complex distribution of responsibilities within the German state organisation. In any case, the further opening of the German cybersecurity policy towards more active cyber defence measures and the creation of corresponding legal regulations and practical facilities is likely.

The central question of German politics will continue to be the right balance between ensuring cybersecurity and national security on the one hand and protecting privacy and civil liberties on the other. This question will become apparent in the discussions about data retention by providers, the law enforcement and intelligence rights and the handling of vulnerabilities. It would be a welcome development if the country were to introduce its approaches, which have emerged from intensive national discussions, more strongly into the international debate. Germany can make a significant contribution to the development and formulation of a balance between preventive cyber protection and reasonable active defence measures. The same applies to the pervasive experience with public-private partnerships covering many aspects of cybersecurity, which Germany could use as an example in international policy reflections.

The UN resolution "The right to privacy in the digital age", which came into effect following German and Brazilian action in 2013, shows, like the German work in the UN GGE, that Germany has the potential to successfully engage in the international community for common approaches to tackling the challenges of digitisation.

Printed in the United States
By Bookmasters